STUDIES IN ANTHROPOLOGICAL METHOD

General Editors

GEORGE AND LOUISE SPINDLER

Stanford University

HOW TO LEARN AN UNWRITTEN LANGUAGE

HOW TO LEARN
AN UNWRITTEN
LANGUAGE

SARAH C. GUDSCHINSKY

Summer Institute of Linguistics
Santa Ana, California

HOLT, RINEHART AND WINSTON
New York   Chicago   San Francisco   Atlanta
Dallas   Montreal   Toronto   London

FOREWORD

ABOUT THE SERIES

Anthropology has been, since the turn of the century, a significant influence shaping Western thought. It has brought into proper perspective the position of our culture as one of many and has challenged universalistic and absolutistic assumptions and beliefs about the proper condition of man. Anthropology has been able to make this contribution mainly through its descriptive analyses of non-Western ways of life. Only in the last decades of its comparatively short existence as a science have anthropologists developed systematic theories about human behavior in its transcultural dimensions, and only very recently have anthropological techniques of data collection and analysis become explicit and in some instances replicable.

Teachers of anthropology have been handicapped by the lack of clear, authoritative statements of how anthropologists collect and analyze relevant data. The results of fieldwork are available in the ethnographies and they can be used to demonstrate cultural diversity and integration, social control, religious behavior, marriage customs, and the like, but clear, systematic statements about how the facts are gathered and interpreted are rare in the literature readily available to students. Without this information the alert reader of anthropological literature is left uninformed about the process of our science, knowing only of the results. This is an unsatisfying state of affairs for both the student and the instructor.

This series is designed to help solve this problem. Each study in the series focuses upon manageable dimensions of modern anthropological methodology. Each one demonstrates significant aspects of the processes of gathering, ordering, and interpreting data. Some are highly selected dimensions of methodology. Others are concerned with the whole range of experience involved in studying a total society. These studies are written by professional anthropologists who have done fieldwork and have made significant contributions to the science of man and his works. In them the authors explain how they go about this work, and to what end. We think they will be helpful to students who want to know what processes of inquiry and ordering stand behind the formal, published results of anthropology.

ABOUT THE AUTHOR

Sarah Gudschinsky, literacy coordinator of the Summer Institute of Linguistics and its affiliate corporation, Wycliffe Bible Translators, is an educator turned linguist. She received a B.S. degree in education from Central Michigan University, and taught in Michigan's rural elementary schools for several years before becoming interested in linguistics. Her early fieldwork included linguistic investigation and literacy work with the Mazatec tribe of Mexico. After completing a Ph.D. in linguistics at the University of Pennsylvania, she has served as chairman of the Technical Studies Department of the Brazil branch of the Summer Institute of Linguistics. Dr. Gudschinsky has taught linguistics at the Summer Institute at the University of Oklahoma, at the University of Brasilia in Brazil, and as visiting professor at the University of London's University College. She is the author of *Handbook of Literacy, Proto-Propotecan: A Comparative Study of Popolocan and Mixtecan,* and a number of articles on linguistics and literacy.

ABOUT THE BOOK

Dr. Gudschinsky provides in this brief volume a concise introductory course in linguistics specifically directed at the learning of language in the field, and intended for the linguistically naïve student. At each step problems are presented and the analytic techniques required to solve them are explained. The reader is constantly reminded of the cultural relevance of language and the methods used to study it.

The first chapter provides an orientation for the student going into the field. Chapter 2 is a succinct statement of the grammatical points a student will have to master. This is presented in an extraordinarily clear manner that will be understandable to students with little or no linguistic background. Chapter 3 includes a detailed explanation of how to learn vocabulary within the grammatical framework. The author points out the pitfalls of loan-translation from English, emphasizing that words have one or several areas of meaning and that vocabulary must be learned in context. Chapter 4 is a brief presentation of phonological theory. Though technical terminology is kept at an absolute minimum, a new student will need some expert help if he is to understand the full implications of this chapter. Chapter 5 has the practical goal of flexibility in the production of sounds. Articulation positions, manner of articulation, modifications in point of articulation, voicing, glottal stop, secondary articulation, clicks and glottalized sounds, vowels, and, finally, pitch and rhythm are presented in that order. Exercises abound and are clearly presented, enabling the student to follow the directions literally, and making it possible for the motivated student to learn many of the basic lessons without a teacher. These five chapters are followed by a listing of practical considerations for the choice of a tape recorder to be used in linguistic fieldwork, a chart of consonants and vowels, a bibliography of books and pamphlets on language learning, and various introductory works on linguistics.

As an introduction to practical linguistics this volume is unparalleled. A linguistically naïve student who reads this book will know what he must control in order to learn a language in the field with linguistic methods. The student who studies the book by himself and follows the exercises through faithfully will have gained some of the basic skills necessary for such learning. The sharp, succinct quality of Dr. Gudschinsky's presentation and the eminently sensible ordering of exercises and conceptual points will also be a great aid to instruction in linguistic courses at both the introductory and more advanced levels. The volume is so specific that it will also be useful as a field manual to remind the student of essential procedures and purposes.

GEORGE AND LOUISE SPINDLER
General Editors
Stanford, July 1967

The editors gratefully acknowledge the help of Dr. Edith C. Trager in the review of the manuscript and the preparation of the foreword.

PREFACE

When I agreed to write *How to Learn an Unwritten Language,* it seemed like a very simple thing to do. During the past eight years I have advised more than thirty linguistic research teams on how to begin learning and analyzing an unwritten language, and have supervised their fieldwork. Writing the book would be only a matter of putting on paper what I had been saying to my beginning colleagues.

There have been severe and unexpected problems in this simple process, however. My colleagues are embryonic linguists. They have had a minimum of two very intensive summer courses in linguistic analysis and theory. For them, learning to use the language is an integral part of producing a professional description of it. This book is designed for an audience of linguistically naïve anthropology students as preparation for anthropological fieldwork in which control of the local language is necessary. Instead of building on a measure of linguistic competence, I find myself obliged to provide what is essentially a vastly simplified introduction to linguistics. I have found it exceedingly difficult to provide enough linguistic theory to be useful without overwhelming the beginner with more than he can absorb. It has proved even more difficult to be simple enough to be practical without seriously distorting the complexities of language and linguistic analysis.

The simplification has involved limiting the scope of the discussion to everyday conversation, and ignoring many of the more difficult linguistic problems. No attention is paid here to narrative, oratorical, or ceremonial styles nor to variations of social register or geographical dialect.

The form and content of the book are dictated by the following assumptions: (1) learning a language consists of discovering and controlling as automatic habits the phonological, grammatical, and lexical patterns used by its native speakers; (2) a non-linguist can discover in data produced by or elicited from a native speaker, at least the most common and most useful of those patterns; and (3) using a minimum of vocabulary, automatic control can be achieved by intensive practice of the patterns in stimulus and response sequences.

My theoretical orientation is the Tagmemic model of Kenneth L. Pike. This is an appropriate choice for a book on learning an unwritten language inasmuch as the theory has been developed from wide experience in the analysis of such languages, and is currently being tested in fieldwork in both analysis and language learning. The reader who is interested in comparing Tagmemics with other models will find the following introductory materials useful (see Bibliography for full titles): for the generative model of Noam Chomsky see Bach 1964; for two varieties of the older structural model see Hockett 1955, and Hill 1958; for the property grammar model of M. A. K. Halliday see Halliday, McIntosh, and Strevens 1964, Part I; for a further introduction to the Tagmemic model see Elson and Pickett 1962, Longacre 1964, and Pike 1967.

It would be impossible to list all the sources from which I drew in preparing this book, although there is little or nothing in it that is really new. (Most of the basic ideas are found in Sweet 1900, Cummings 1916, Palmer 1917, and Ward 1937.) I acknowledge with gratitude my deep indebtedness to all of the linguists who have pioneered in the problems of analysis and language learning. A more specific appreciation is due my colleagues of the Summer Institute of Linguistics in Mexico and Brazil who have provided the material for the majority of the examples; to Eunice Burgess, John Crawford, and William Merrifield who have worked through the manuscript correcting errors and assessing its usefulness for beginners; and to LaVera Betts, Loys Mundy, Jo Ann Conrad, and others who have spent long hours typing and proofreading.

SARAH C. GUDSCHINSKY

Santa Ana, Calif.
July 1967

CONTENTS

HOW TO LEARN AN UNWRITTEN LANGUAGE

Introduction

WHEN AN ANTHROPOLOGIST undertakes the study of a little-known culture, he is quite likely to find himself working with a group whose language is equally little known. All that he wishes to study, however, is intimately linked to the language. Observed behavior cannot be understood apart from the verbalizations of participants and local observers. (Imagine, for example, an Australian aboriginee watching a baseball game without any explanation of what is happening.) The vast bulk of the culture cannot be directly observed within a single field experience; the investigator is dependent upon anecdotes, explanations, and extrapolations provided by his informants. Analysis of many aspects of the culture requires a knowledge of special terms for special categories, and for this a translation is not a useful substitute. An understanding of religious concepts, for example, may be dependent upon a knowledge of categories of supernatural beings or phenomena, each with its generic term; an analysis of a kinship system is dependent upon a knowledge of the kin terms themselves, as a clue to categories and relationships. The anthropologist is helpless, therefore, unless he can find some means of communication with the community he wishes to study.

It is tempting to suppose that the problem of communication can be solved by using an interpreter, or by finding bilingual informants. An informant, in the sense used here, is a native speaker of the language with whom the student can work, eliciting language data, checking his understanding or performance in the language, or practicing conversation. The informant may be presumed to be bilingual or partially bilingual, speaking a trade language or national language in addition to his own native language. This assumption is based on a prior assumption that no anthropology student without linguistic training is likely to attempt the study of a culture in which all the participants are monolingual speakers of a language that he does not know.

Neither of these solutions is satisfactory, however. Even the best interpreter hinders the investigator's rapport with his informants, and is an unreliable channel for information. The investigator is therefore limited to working with those members of the community with whom his interpreter has rapport, and those aspects of the culture that the informant is willing to discuss with the interpreter. He is further limited by the interpreter's imperfect understanding of his purpose, and by any imperfection in the interpreter's control of one or the other of the languages involved.

Working directly with bilingual informants is almost as unsatisfactory. It is the author's experience that the members of a primitive community are frequently unable to discuss their culture adequately in a second language. Many of their concepts have no equivalents in the second language; even if such equivalents existed, those who have never thought about these things in the second language find it awkward, if not impossible, to talk about them. In communities where there is considerable contact with a more highly developed industrial culture, the informant may be embarrassed to talk in the trade language about elements of his culture which are the target of ridicule by his more "civilized" neighbors. In any case, he may be reluctant to speak about intimate matters in the language that he associates with business or political contacts. Furthermore, bilinguals are frequently atypical; the very contacts through which they have learned fluency in a second language may have cut them off from full participation in their own culture. This will cause them to be rated among the least satisfactory informants.

A thorough anthropological study carried on over a number of years requires a fluent knowledge of the language. It is not surprising that many outstanding cultural anthropologists such as Boas, Sapir, and Kroeber have also been outstanding linguists. It is reasonable to expect that the total professional preparation of an anthropologist should include a solid grounding in linguistics. Many anthropology students, however, do their first fieldwork (perhaps as the basis for a thesis or dissertation) without such linguistic preparation. To such students it may seem wasteful to try to learn the language on a field trip of nine or ten months, as complete control is obviously out of the question. There are, however, decided advantages in making language learning the top priority for half or more of such a short field term, and to continue it as a secondary activity throughout the entire field project. First, the attempt to learn the language provides immediate rapport with the people; it is a common experience that efforts at learning and direct communication stimulate friendliness and a spirit of helpfulness. Second, even very modest success will permit the investigator to record crucial data, such as kin terms, in the language. Third, several months of intensive language study should enable the investigator to make more adequate use of interpreters or bilingual informants. Some knowledge of the language will enable him to know, or at least guess, when he is being wildly misunderstood, or when he is receiving information that has been badly distorted in the translation.

Language study and practice give excellent opportunities for observation and participation in community activities with no appearance of direct prying. Constant contact with the people enables the investigator to develop rapport with many different potential informants, and to assess their varying gifts. As the language reflects the rest of the culture, insights into the language and the thought patterns it expresses will help in the final understanding of the culture as a whole.

This book is designed to aid the fieldworker with little or no linguistic background in making a beginning in learning a language without a teacher or textbook. The practical suggestions may also be a useful supplement to linguistic courses which provide a survey of the field, or emphasize methods of linguistic analysis with little attention to problems of language learning.

1

Preparation for Language Learning

EVERYONE READING this book has already demonstrated his ability to learn a language, as he has attained adult control of his mother tongue. Anyone who has learned one language certainly has the ability to learn another. However, some handicaps that an adult brings to language learning may frustrate this native ability. The automatic control of one language interferes with acquiring adequate control of another; the more automatic a habit, the more difficult it is to substitute a different habit. The adult's deep distaste for making a fool of himself or for being laughed at may hinder his progress in learning a new language, as mistakes will be an inevitable part of his early attempts to speak.

Many of the exercises in the following sections (especially the phonetics exercises) are intended to give the student conscious control of his English habits. It is assumed that conscious control of one's own habits is a first step toward conscious control of new patterns, which in turn can be made automatic habits by intensive practice.

It is possible, through library research, to reduce the task of learning a new language before actually going to the field. Each area of the world, or each of the great language families, has certain characteristics which are peculiar to it. There is no point, for example, in learning how to make clicks if one is going to work with a South American Indian language in which clicks do not usually occur. On the other hand, it would be foolish to plan to learn a language of India without some previous practice in the making of retroflexed consonants and voiced, aspirated stops.

The research might include the following topics: (1) an acquaintance with the phonological types to be expected in the languages of that particular area or language family; (2) similar investigation of the grammatical types; (3) acquaintance with the cultural and physical setting so far as it is known; and (4) a search for specific descriptions of the language to be studied. There is a surprising amount of material published by missionaries or travelers on languages that are still otherwise largely unknown. Such material is useful as background; but it is not wise to attempt to memorize anything that one has not heard spoken. Premature practice of this sort results in bad habits that are difficult to correct.

3

The student's shyness or reserve is quite a different problem. If he chooses to maintain his dignity and pride, refusing to talk until he can do so without error, he is not likely to learn to talk well. If, on the other hand, he chooses to ignore his embarrassment and to talk in spite of feeling foolish, he will usually find that people are genuinely sympathetic and helpful although they are amused by his mistakes. If the foreigner laughs with them, people tend to remember his friendliness rather than his errors; but if he is stiff and embarrassed they may consider him unfriendly.

There is no way to learn to talk except by talking. If the student knows only two or three words he should use them on every possible occasion and in every possible context; he should also attempt to find other words to use with them in order to enlarge his repertory. In this instance the sociable person has the advantage. The natural chatterbox will use all the language at his command, and then reach for more from sheer inability to stop talking. The introvert, or the man of few words, must deliberately develop some social characteristics. He must learn to chat whether or not he is really in the mood for conversation and whether or not he has anything to say. There are many people who are untalkative in English, but who are voluble in the languages in which they work. This appears to be the result of deliberate choice made in the early stages of learning. Fortunately, most languages and cultures have many contexts in which chatting is acceptable, giving the student ample opportunity for the kind of language practice that he needs. In some cultures, etiquette actually requires repetitive conversation: "What are you doing?" "I'm hoeing corn." "Are you hoeing corn?" "Yes, I'm hoeing corn." "You hoe very well." "No, I don't hoe very well." In most cultures the student can carry on lengthy conversations with children. If he is fortunate he will find a few imaginative ones who will assume a variety of roles and so extend the usefulness of the practice.

Field Procedures

There has been considerable confusion about the way in which adults learn a new language. It is sometimes assumed that they will learn best if they merely hear and mimic as a child does, leaving the pattern making to their unconscious learning. On the other hand, it is sometimes assumed that the adult learns best by memorizing rules and vocabulary first, and then practicing the patterns as examples of the rules. One reason for this confusion and difference of opinion may be that people vary enormously in the way they react to language and, perhaps, in the way that they learn. A few people appear to be natural mimics; they apprehend, react to, and remember new language patterns almost immediately. Such people do not have to analyze the language in order to perfect their speaking ability. Others are unable to use language patterns until they are aware of them explicitly in terms of conscious insights into the relationships involved.

The viewpoint of this book is eclectic: the necessity for listening, mimicry, and practice in living context is emphasized. Analysis is presented as a tool for discovering the patterns to be learned and the contexts in which they should be drilled. In using these materials, the born mimic should be careful to exploit the analytical techniques to the extent that they are useful to him; the desk-bound introvert should force himself to make social contacts and should engage in mimicry, thus avoiding the danger of an elaborate written analysis that does not contribute to his actual facility in conversation.

In general, a language-learning program in the field should include all or most of the following elements every day:

1. Periods of listening to normal conversation between native speakers, making an effort to understand and to contribute. In the early stages, the ability to catch the drift of a conversation constitutes success. Later, the learner should be able to follow the detail of what is being said. His earliest contributions may be no more than the culturally acceptable indications of continued attention, or the *yes* of agreement. Eventually he should be able to participate as a member of the group.

Opportunities for observing and participating in this kind of conversation may sometimes be found in purely social gatherings. They are probably more frequent, however, in the context of shared work (for example, women at the water hole or men in the harvest field).

2. Many conversations with individuals. The student should seek out opportunities for conversation, and should make a point of talking with everyone with whom he has direct contact. He should also make conversational partners of curious children who have been watching him. If he has arrangements for formal study with a language informant, he should spend some part of this time in free conversation.

3. Several brief periods of listening intensively to materials recorded on magnetic tape, and subsequently mimicking them. These materials should include both connected text and word lists.

The texts should be short enough to be repeated several times in a single listening period. The advantage of listening to text is that the recorder faithfully repeats such things as intonation pattern and rhythm often enough for the student to feel it and to mimic it. This is not true in free conversation where patterns may shift too rapidly for the student to absorb them. Also, in using the tape recorder he can concentrate his entire attention on hearing and mimicry without the confusion of trying to follow difficult content or trying to plan something to say.

Listening to recorded lists of words is of special value for distinguishing tone, stress, and length patterns. Listening for these things should be alternated with lists in which the feature under focus is identical, and lists in which there are contrastively different sets. In a language in which stress placement is important in recognizing words, the first arrangement might be three lists, one with stress on the first syllable, one with stress on the second syllable, and one with stress on the third syllable. The second arrangement might be lists containing three words, in which the three words in each list have stress on the first syllable, the second syllable, and the third syllable, respectively. (Lesson material that is being memorized as suggested in points 6 and 7 might also be recorded for these listening periods.)

4. Gathering of new data. There are three sources of new data: (a) The student should write down any utterance he hears, and the context in which it was said. (b) If he has an informant, he may elicit data from the informant. (c) He may record texts on magnetic tape. It is the unelicited data (points a and c) that is most likely to be accurate and smooth; elicited data is likely to be wooden and foreign, carrying something of the flavor of the language in which it was elicited. On the other hand, some details of the language can be studied and understood much more rapidly if the crucial examples are elicited in a patterned way.

5. Processing of data. It is vital that each day's collection of data be processed at

once. A backlog of material that has not been looked at carefully becomes a serious source of frustration, and paralyzes further activity. This means that all tape-recorded material should be transcribed as soon as possible. Each utterance that has been heard in a natural conversation and written in a data book should be analyzed and classified that same day. Each utterance elicited from an informant should be planned to illuminate some particular problem or to produce an example of a particular pattern.

6. Organization of lessons. At least the nucleus of what the student learns each day should be a planned lesson. A typical lesson should include material for drilling the sound system (points 3 and 8), one or more, grammatical patterns to be practiced until they become habit-forming, and some vocabulary items to be memorized within the grammatical context. Material should be organized into lessons as it is processed.

7. Drill and memorization of a new lesson, and review of old lessons. Each lesson should be of a size that can be learned thoroughly in one day. This means that each day the student will have the satisfaction of learning something new, and knowing that he has made progress. The lessons should be reviewed frequently, and not counted as fully learned until they can be used in free conversation at normal speech speed.

8. Drill on the sound system with an informant. Every day there should be a brief intensive period of contrastive listening and mimicry, especially of those sounds that are different from English sounds. This should not be a tape drill, as most inexpensive portable tape recorders do not provide sufficient fidelity for distinguishing all the phonetic sounds (for example, s and f; t and glottal stop). Contrastive listening means listening for particular sounds and, especially, listening to pairs of words in which similar but contrastively different sounds occur. In this drill the adult student is doing consciously and intentionally what the child does unconsciously in his hours of repetitive babble.

Use of Informants

It is the function of an informant to supply utterances from his own language, not to make pronouncements as to how the language works, or why certain forms are used. Utterances may be elicited by asking in the trade language, "How do you say _____ ?" This method has some inherent dangers; in replying to this sort of question many bilinguals adapt to their own language some of the features of the trade language (for example, word order and kinds of word formation). If the student is asking for patterned sets of data (for example, a paradigm such as I go, you go, he goes), the informant may fill out the pattern giving forms that can be constructed but which are not in fact used in the language. On the other hand, if the informant is not very imaginative, he may refuse to give some perfectly normal form or sequence because he cannot at the moment think of a context in which he would use it. All of this means that material elicited through the trade language must be treated with great care. The wise student will check all elicited material against native text to see if the same patterns also occur where contamination from the trade language is not a factor.

The kinds of data that can most usefully be elicited through the trade language include: phrases essential for doing business; question forms; missing members of paradigms; new expansions or varieties of sentences; and new vocabulary items. The trade language has only limited usefulness in eliciting such things as verb tenses and aspects and person markers, as these things may be so different from what occurs in the trade language that they can not be equated.

When the student is able to control a small nucleus of the language, the task of eliciting from the informant in his own language, rather than by translation, is much more rewarding. In this type of eliciting, the student may (1) ask questions in the language to find out the form of an acceptable response (Student: "What are you doing?" Informant: "Studying."); (2) ask questions about pictures ("What is this boy doing?" "Why is the girl sitting there?"); and (3) provide a sentence from his data and ask the informant to expand it by adding a word or phrase such as "yesterday" or "for his brother." This type of expansion may produce some of the tenses and aspects that cannot be obtained by direct questioning or translation.

The student can use the informant to check utterances that he has made up by analogy with the utterances in his data. It is not wise to ask the informant, "Can I say _____ ?" If the student and the informant are not focussing on the same part of the utterance, the answer to that question may be quite misleading. The informant may mean, "No, we never say that the moon is yellow," while the student understands him to mean, "No, adjectives do not occur with verbal endings." The better form is to ask, "If I say _____ what would it mean?" The informant's answer, "I don't know" or "What did you say?" may mean that there are too many gross errors of some sort for comprehension. The informant asking, "Did you say _____ ?" probably constitutes a correction, and should be listened to carefully and compared with the original utterance. If the informant answers, "It means _____ ," which differs from what the student intended to say, it is a clue to patterns or use of patterns which have been overlooked. If the informant answers, "It means _____ ," which agrees with what the student intended, this is confirmation of his understanding of the pattern he is testing. In such testing, sensitivity to the informant is especially important.

A rather different kind of checking involves asking the informant to repeat a list of words or phrases that can be checked for similarity or difference of certain features (for example, lists of words having the same tone pattern, stress pattern, initial consonant, or other feature, versus sets of words having contrastively different tone patterns, stress patterns, or initial consonants). Care should be taken not to require more repetitions than the informant can give naturally. Recording such lists for private listening can reduce the number of repetitions needed from the informant.

Use of Tape Recorders

A tape recorder is an especially valuable tool for fieldwork, functioning as a mechanical memory which can repeat endlessly what it has recorded. It has three primary values for the student learning a language. First, it permits him to gather data at the normal speed of speech without the distortion that results from asking the informant to speak at dictation speed. Second, it provides him with models for listening or mimicry that can be used indefinitely. Third, it permits him to hear his own voice and to pinpoint his problems or successes in learning.

Awkward manipulation of the recorder may sharply reduce its usefulness. Therefore, the student should familiarize himself with the machine at home before taking it to the field, using his friends or fellow students as informants until his technique has become smooth. (See the Appendix for suggestions about recording equipment.)

In the field, the student may find that people are afraid of the recorder. One way of overcoming such fear is for the student to use the machine himself without comment. If people see him recording his own voice and listening to it, their curiosity may gradually overcome their fear. Sooner or later some of the bolder ones may want to hear their voices. It is important, however, that they should not feel pressured to do something that they are afraid of. On the other hand, it is not wise to record conversations without the knowledge and consent of the participants.

Even after the people have become accustomed to the machine, it is unlikely that anyone will respond very effectively if he is handed the microphone and told to say something. This has a devasting effect in any language. Good results require a triggering audience or situation. Among the possibilities for collecting data on a recorder are the following:

1. Give the informant pictures on which to comment. These can be planned to elicit material on a particular topic. The pictures can be supplemented by questions such as, "What does this one say?" or "What is that one doing?" The questions, of course, will probably trigger curt responses, rather than full sentences that might be used for initiating conversation.
2. Ask one informant to tell or explain something to another. This is especially effective if the speaker has had an experience that he wants to communicate.
3. Keep the microphone open while stimulating normal conversation between two informants. Such conversation is not useful if there are more than two people entering into the conversation. Neither will it work well if the microphone is not able to pick up the voices of both speakers easily. Such a tape can be edited, and the more useful stretches can be retained to be transcribed and used. False starts or stretches marred by background noise can be discarded.
4. Tape your own conversation with your informant. Note that everything he says which is not a direct answer to the question "How do you say _____ ?" is reliable data. This will provide you with isolated bits such as: response sentences in answer to your questions in the language; questions he asked of you, but without native response; or short paragraphs of narrative or explanation if he elaborated on some point.
5. Ask the tribal storyteller to tape one of his stories. Although this may be of immense value to the anthropologist when he has learned enough to be able to handle it, it is not usually a very useful kind of text for learning to talk, for the following reasons: (a) The stories frequently include special vocabulary or constructions that are not used in normal speech. (b) They are too long to be used for lessons. (c) If small sections are taken from the longer text they may not have the correct intonation and rhythm required for learning them apart from the story.

In addition to new data, any material that the student elicits from the informant can be taped for later use. The student can also have the informant record the material of his lessons on tape. The hand brake can be used to prevent the recording of the student's voice in cases where it is an interruption rather than a help.

In all of this, the mechanics of the recording process should be minimized. It is usually better, for example, to put the microphone where it will pick up the informant's voice easily, but where he does not have to handle it himself.

There are some dangers in the use of a recorder. It is so easy to record material that the student is apt to forget how long it takes to process it, and therefore he is apt to collect more material than he can use. This problem can be avoided by limiting the data collected to what can be used immediately, and by transcribing recorded material either the same day it is recorded or the following day. It takes as long to listen to a tape as it does to record it. It takes at least four times as long to transcribe a tape as it does to record it. The student can judge from the time available to him for processing the tape, how much time it is wise to use for recording.

All transcription should be done with the informant's help, as it is nearly impossible to hear correctly a language that one does not speak fluently. A technique for transcription includes the following steps:

1. Play the tape, stopping at the first natural pause. (It helps to listen to the tape several times before working with the informant, so as to develop an ear for the short pauses as well as for the long ones.)
2. Ask the informant to repeat what he has recorded on the tape. Write it down as he says it, asking for additional repetitions if necessary.
3. Replay the phrase, comparing it with the written version to be sure that nothing has been left out and that there are no major differences.
4. If the informant seems to have added syllables, listen again to see if those syllables were overlooked on the first listening.
5. Pronounce what you have written, and ask the informant if this is what he said. (Notice that this is quite a different question from "Can you say _____ ?")
6. Ask the informant if the written version and the taped version are the same. If he says they are not, ask him why the difference occurred. (Was there an error on the tape?) If he says that they are the same in spite of apparent differences, look for differences between slow pedantic speech and speech at normal speed (for example, the difference between "I am going" and "I'm going," and "Let's go eat" and " 's 'gwit.")
7. After the entire text has been written, ask the informant what the text as a whole means. He is likely to give a shortened summary. Then ask the meaning of each phrase.

$$\boxed{2}$$

Grammar

LEARNING A LANGUAGE has been described (Fries 1945:3) as ". . . first, the mastery of the sound system . . . [and] second, the mastery of the features of arrangement that constitute the structure of the language. . . ." The student should not suppose, however, that he is to master the sound system in some sort of vacuum, and only then go on to the grammatical patterns with which he can communicate. He should begin immediately to discover and to master the grammatical patterns; within these patterns he simultaneously learns to control the sound system and to substitute a variety of vocabulary items. Because of this conviction that the grammatical patterns provide the essential matrix for studying both the sound system and the vocabulary, the grammar is presented first. Of course, in practice, all three must be studied simultaneously; the student cannot talk with grammatical patterns apart from a particular set of vocabulary items within the patterns, nor apart from a particular pronunciation.

In a field situation, the raw material in which patterns are to be discovered is anything the investigator has heard a native speaker say, and has been able to record in a recognizable fashion. The universal method of obtaining such data is the investigator's observation of ordinary speech events in living context. These may be written down as they occur or recorded on magnetic tape for later transcription. Such observation is the only wholly reliable source of patterns to be learned. It must usually be supplemented, however, by material elicited from a bilingual or semibilingual informant.

All grammatical pattern is seen as consisting of sets of positions or slots, and lists of items that are appropriate fillers of each slot. There are basically two complementary techniques for finding such grammatical pattern: (1) stretches of speech can be compared to find repetitions of the same unit with the same meaning; and (2) an informant can be asked to speak a series of utterances in which different forms are substituted for each other in the same position. These techniques are illustrated in Exercise 1 by examples from the Mazatec language of Mexico. In this, and all subsequent examples, the symbols have approximately the value indicated in the phonetic exercises in Chapter 5. The numbers in these examples indicate the relative pitch at which the syllables are spoken. The number 1 indicates high pitch; 2, semihigh pitch; 3, semilow pitch; and 4, low pitch. Combinations of numbers indicate a glide from one pitch to another (for example, 13 is a glide from a high pitch to a semilow pitch).

Exercise 1

Compare the following sentences and identify the unit meaning "person" or "people":

ha^{3}ʔai^{3} čo^{4}ta^{4}	people came
ha^{3}ʔai^{3}kao^{4} hnko^{3} čo^{4}ta^{4} yo^{4}ma^{4}	they came with a sick person
ño^{3} čo^{4}ta^{4} tsa^{3}kʔa^{3}nkʔa^{3}	four people carried him

It is easy to see that čo^{4}ta^{4} is the unit which is repeated in each sentence, and which represents the repeated meaning "people" or "person." Each of the three sentences in this exercise has a different set of positions so that the data as given does not display lists of mutually substitutable items, nor does it show us clearly what the positions are. On the basis of this data, however, it would be possible to elicit from an informant, additional data to define the positions and possible substitution items. In the first sentence, for example, we have identified čo^{4}ta^{4} as "people," and thus ha^{3}ʔai^{3} may mean "came." Therefore, the sentence appears to be made up of a predicate position followed by a subject position. To test this, we might elicit the following forms from an informant:

people went	ki^{43} čo^{4}ta^{4}
people are sick	ti^{1}mʔe^{3} čo^{4}ta^{4}
people dance	ti^{1}te^{2} čo^{4}ta^{4}

This data confirms the hypothesis that the original sentence represented a predicate position plus a subject position. It also gives a list of fillers for the predicate position; these can be identified as ki^{43}, "went"; ti^{1}mʔe^{3}, "is sick"; and ti^{1}te^{2}, "is dancing."

In the third sentence of the original data there is the expression "four people" which appears to be represented by ño^{3} čo^{4}ta^{4}. To test this hypothesis, one might elicit the following from an informant:

one person	hnko^{3} čo^{4}ta^{4}
two persons	hao^{2} čo^{4}ta^{4}
three persons	hạ^{2} čo^{4}ta^{4}
four people	ño^{3} čo^{4}ta^{4}

This data defines a position which may be filled by the following numbers: hnko^{3}, "one"; hao^{2}, "two"; hạ^{2}, "three"; and ño,^{3} "four." Further data may be elicited to indicate what forms can be substituted for čo^{4}ta^{4} in this construction:

one person	hnko^{3} čo^{4}ta^{4}
one snake	hnko^{3} ye^{4}
one boy	hnko^{4} ti^{3}

The fillers of a position may be phrases of more than one word, as are the fillers of the subject position in the following sentences:

ti¹m²ę³ ño⁴³ čo⁴ta⁴	Four people are sick.
ti¹m²ę³ hnko³ ti³	One boy is sick.
ti¹m²ę³ hą³ ye⁴	Three snakes are sick.

There may also be positions within a word. In the following examples there are two positions within the noun word: (1) a stem position and (2) an affix position which is filled by the following forms indicating the person of a possessor: -na,⁴ "my"; -li,⁴ "your"; -le,⁴ "his"; and nąi⁴ hi,⁴ "our."

ti¹m²ę³ ti³ną⁴	My boy is sick.
ti¹m²ę³ ti³li⁴	Your boy is sick.
ti¹m²ę³ ti³le⁴	His boy is sick.
ti¹m²ę³ ti³nąi⁴hi⁴	Our boy is sick.

A language is a unified whole, and all of its parts are intimately interrelated. There is some sense in which to learn a language at all it is necessary to learn all of it at once. In practice, however, the learner must focus on one part or aspect of the language at a time. He keeps the whole in view by a frequent shift of focus. In the following sections, the student is provided with a review of some kinds of grammatical structure he may find in the language he is studying. These are presented in an order that should be useful for investigation and learning in the field. This order is not rigid, of course, and should be modified to meet specific problems.

Discussion here is limited to everyday conversation. It is assumed that good control of a language on a conversational level can be expanded to include other styles.

Opening and Closing Conversation

If the investigator is to be accepted in the community, one of the first things he must learn is the culturally acceptable way to begin and end conversations. There may be particular greeting forms required, or there may be some element of nonverbal behavior (the polite cough that notifies a Munduruku householder in Brazil that a guest has arrived, or the long silence with which a visitor waits for his host's attention in some other Brazilian tribes). This nonverbal behavior may be fully as important as or more important than the linguistic forms. It is probable that the prescribed forms will differ with the cultural setting. Initiating a house visit, for example, may be quite different from a greeting on the road.

A procedure for choosing the material to be learned is as follows:

1. For each different cultural context of social encounter (meeting on the road, going for a visit, transacting business arrangements, working together in the field or house) record typical greetings and closings. Include in the record the nonverbal behavior or gestures, as well as the words used. Make the linguistic recording on magnetic tape, if feasible, so that it can be mimicked.

2. From the recorded material, choose those sequences that are most commonly used or those that are most essential for your own activities.

3. Memorize these sequences and use them on every possible occasion. Continue to listen carefully to native participants so that you may correct your own pronunciation and usage.

Exercise 2

Examine the following examples of greetings and farewells from Isthmus Zapotec of Mexico (Pickett 1960:88–89).

Greeting (brief street encounter)

ži'tálžǎ	How are you?
ga'lán. 'liʔi yaʔ	Fine. And you?
ga'lán. tam'byén.	Fine too.

Greeting (home visit)

'hú	Yoohoo.
'byúʔu	Come in.
'mǎpekǎ	I'm coming.

Farewell: (home visit)

'bwěno. 'yanna.	Well. I'm going now.
'bwěno. sika'ru 'čeúʔ	Ok. May you go well.
sika'ru 'gyáʔanúʔ	May you stay well.

Conversational Exchange

Within a conversation, the unit which is most useful for language learning is an exchange involving at least one utterance by each of two speakers—usually a stimulus and a response. Each language has its own characteristic patterns for such exchanges. Note, for example, the contrast between English and Portuguese in a typical question and answer sequence.

English
Stimulus: "Does the bus stop here?"
Response: "Yes, it does." *or* "No, it doesn't."

Portuguese
Stimulus: *O onibus para aquí?* "The bus stops here?"
Response: *Para, sim.* "(It) stops, yes."
or
Não para, não. "Not (it) stops, no."

In English the affirmative (yes) or negative (no) is required, usually followed by the substitute forms for the subject (it) and the predicate (does). In Portuguese, on the other hand, such substitute forms do not occur. Rather, the verb is repeated in either positive form (*para,* "it stops") or negative form (*não para,* "it doesn't stop"), followed by the affirmative (*sim*) or negative (*não*). A native speaker of either language can probably think of contexts in which some other answer would be acceptable (for example, "No, it doesn't stop *here*" or "No, the *bus* doesn't stop"). To repeat the entire clause, however—subject, predicate, and locational—would be awkward and unnatural in either language. An American is not likely to respond to the question, "Does the bus stop here?" by saying "The bus stops here"; it would also be unlikely that a Brazilian would answer the question by saying, "O onibus para aquí."

In most languages there are several kinds of stimulus–response units. Of these, the beginner's most pressing need is probably question and answer sequences. He is almost certain to be asked many questions, especially during his early days in the community, and he should be able to ask questions in order to be sociable and to elicit both linguistic and anthropological data.

Most languages make a distinction between at least two kinds of questions, a request for confirmation ("Did John say he was going?"), which calls for an affirmative or negative answer which may echo the question, and a content question ("What did John say?" or "Where did John go?"), which calls for an answer which complements the question. The example given at the beginning of this section is a request for confirmation.

Of these two types of questions, content questions are probably the most useful starting point. The student may use the following steps in finding, analyzing, organizing, and learning question and answer sequences.

1. Take a model for question and answer sequences from natural text. (See Chapter 1 for techniques of gathering text.)

2. Analyze the model, either by comparing it with other examples from the text or by eliciting substitutions from an informant. This analysis should distinguish the major positions in the questions, and the kind of items that can be substituted. The following English series isolates the position for the question words "where" "what" and "how" and the positions for subjects and predicates within questions such as: "Where do the children play?" "What do the children play?" "How do the children play?" "Where do the children sleep?" "Where do the men sleep?" "Where do the visitors sleep?"

3. Choose a set of questions based on one question word with a small number of substitutions of subject and verb, and practice until each of these can be asked smoothly enough to be understood by a native speaker. The reason for limiting this step to a single question word is that each question word may call for a different kind of response (for example, "where" usually requires a locative response, "when" requires a time expression, and "who" requires a noun phrase). In practicing the questions, each repetition should be triggered by an appropriate imagined or dramatized situation. Do not use English or a trade language as a crutch. Refuse to think in English; let the situation itself stimulate the appropriate utterance.

4. Use the questions in real life situations to elicit a variety of responses.

5. From the elicited responses choose those that can be used immediately and repeatedly. Do not overload your lesson with too many questions or with too many responses to any one question.

6. Memorize these question and answer sequences. Practice them intensively with a colleague, spouse, native informant, native child, or visitor. Have the informant record them on magnetic tape, and then make tape loops for private mimicry and practice. Use the sequence on all possible occasions. Take the initiating part wherever there is opportunity. Keep alert for questions of others to which you can respond. A typical lesson might include something like the following:

Where do you live?	Over there.
Where do you live?	On the hill.
Where do you live?	On the river bank.
Where do you sleep?	Over there.
Where do you sleep?	In that hammock.
Where do you eat?	Over there.
Where do you eat?	By the fire.

These steps should be repeated for each of the question words. A language may be expected to have some way of asking the following: "when?" "where?" "who did it?" "to whom was it done?" "how was it done?" "why was it done?" and "what is being done?"

In proceeding in this fashion, the student must be very sensitive to the culture in which he is working. It may well be that some questions are impolite. In this case, of course, he will begin with sequences that are more acceptable. There may also be types of responses that are appropriate in different situations. In Mazatec, for example, the question hñą^1 ti$^{2?}$ mi^2 ("Where are you going?") may be answered in a polite friendly fashion by ną^{3}nta^1 ti^{2}fia^3 ("I'm going to the water hole"); in polite but less friendly fashion by thị^1 hñą^3 ti^{2}fia^3 ("There is someplace I'm going"); and in a relatively unfriendly fashion by li^{2}hñą^3 ("Nowhere"). The student will want to make careful choice of the responses he memorizes for his own use, though he may also practice the others so as to recognize them when he hears them.

There may be some questions to be learned without responses; these are questions that the student wishes to use in order to elicit information (for example, "What does _____ mean?," "How do you say _____?," and the like). These should be set up and practiced as in steps 1, 2, and 3.

Most languages have a variety of stimulus–response sequences in addition to question and answer sequences. Each of these can be studied, using the same six steps outlined above. Among the more common types that the student might expect to find are the following: (1) requests and acknowledgment followed by appropriate action: "Will you please shut the door" (request); "Certainly" (response and action); and (2) affirmation and acknowledgment: "John is sick this morning" (affirmation); "That's too bad" (acknowledgment).

There may also be sequences in which one of the speakers is required to speak more than once. In Mazatec, for example, echo sequences are common.

Stimulus:	hme¹ ši³ ti³ñ² ai²³	What are you doing?
Response:	ti² si⁴³ te⁴³ nia¹³	I'm making tortillas.
Echo question:	²a³ti³ni²te⁴³ni¹³	Are you making tortillas?
Echo response:	hao³ ti²si⁴³te⁴³nia¹³ nio⁴	Yes, I'm making tortillas.

In another common type of sequence, the second speaker's contribution serves as both response and further stimulus, so that the exchange includes three utterances.

Stimulus:	Do you have your ticket?
Response and Stimulus:	No, have you?
Response:	Yes, I have.

Word Structures: Person, Tense, Aspect, Mode

The student learning a variety of conversational sequences will soon notice that the stimulus and response must be matched as to persons referred to, the time or kind of action, and perhaps many other features. Notice, for example, the reciprocal pairing of subjects in the following English examples: (1) "How are you?" "I'm fine." (2) "Are you all going?" "Yes, we are." (3) "What do I need?" "You need a pencil and paper." (4) "How will we get there?" "You can take the bus." (5) "Where is John?" "He is in the house." (6) "When will the girls get here?" "They are coming on the five o'clock bus."

In the following set of English examples, there is a matching of tense or mode: (1) "When did John go?" "He went early this morning"; (2) "Where should I go?" "You should try the main office first"; and (3) "Is he sleeping?" "No, he's eating his dinner."

This kind of matching is discussed under word structures, as in many languages the categories of person of subject or object, and the categories of tense, aspect, or mode, are marked by verbal prefixes or suffixes. One type of Mazatec verbs, for example, have a suffix marking the person:

²a³ me³li² na⁴nta¹	Do you (singular) want water?
me³na³	I want.

Mazatec verbs of another type may have the person of subject marked in several places in the verb. Notice the contrasting forms of the following paradigm:

I am working.	ti² si⁴³ ša¹³
You are working.	ti² ni² šai¹³
He is working.	ti¹ si¹ ša¹

There are differences on each syllable. The first and second persons have *ti²* where the third person has *ti¹*. The second person has *ni²* where the first and third persons both have *si*, but with different tone—43 in the first person but 1 in the third person. All three persons have *ša*[1]; the first and second persons have an additional tone [3]; and the second person also has an additional vowel, *i*.

In Bororo of Brazil, the subject is marked by a prefix on the verb stem and the tense is marked by a suffix:

i-tu-mëde	I will go.
i-tu-re	I went.
i-tu-nïre	I am going.
a-tu-re	You went.
e-tu-re	He went.
a-tu-mëde	You will go.

In general, it is relatively easy for the student to elicit the persons from an informant. An elicited paradigm (I _____, you _____, he _____) is useful for finding the positions in which person markers occur, and identifying the forms that mark each person. It is not useful, however, to memorize such a paradigm. All memorization should be done in natural speaking contexts, so that any form that is heard triggers a normal response rather than the next item on an artificial list.

The student should be aware of some of the ways in which person systems may differ from the Indo-European systems with which he is familiar: (1) In many languages there is no special marker for a third person subject or object (he, she, it); there are only markers for the first person (I) and the second person (you). (2) Many languages have different forms for a first person plural (we) that includes the hearer (you), and a first person plural that excludes the hearer. (3) In many languages there is a difference between dual (two persons involved) and plural (more than two persons involved). (4) Some languages mark both the subject and the object in the verb; others mark just the subject or just the object. (5) Some languages use different person markers for different classes of nouns (for example, animate versus inanimate, or long versus round versus tall). (6) Focus or emphasis on subject or object may be marked by using a different set of person markers.

The systems of tense, aspect, and mode are often very complex. They usually differ so much from the usage of an Indo-European trade language that they cannot be elicited by translation. For example, some languages differentiate between complete and incomplete action without reference to time. Other languages mark a contrast between the present (in either time or space) and the remote (in past time, future time, or geographical space).

Fortunately, the student can learn and use the paired verb forms even though he cannot find their exact meaning. Knowing that the system is likely to be very different from that of his own language, he can develop sensitivity to the contexts in which the different forms are used. A habit of jotting down whatever he hears people around him saying will help him. He should also be quick to recognize corrections from his informant, or from other participants in a conversation. Memorizing taped conversation would be of special help in this connection, if it were possible to stimulate and tape a number of brief exchanges within different social groups.

While working on person markers of verbs, the student may find it useful to learn the possession markers of nouns as well, as these are often the same or closely related forms. The possessed nouns ("my hand," "your hand") can probably be elicited in paradigms. Care should be taken, however, to avoid confusion between "my" and "your." If the student says "my hand," holding up his own, the informant is likely to respond with the form meaning "your hand." The student may already have some possessives in his earliest data, as body parts and kin terms often have obligatory possession. The forms which mark such obligatory possession may be different from the forms marking optional possession. It may also be that some nouns cannot be possessed; in the Carib languages of Brazil, for example, one cannot say "my dog" or "my cow" but only "my pet."

The possessed nouns should be learned within the frames that are already familiar. "Where does your father live?" may be substituted for "Where do you live?" Subsequently, a type of question and answer sequence involving possessive relationships might be added to the lessons. These might include the question for information ("Whose boat is this?"), and the question for confirmation ("Is this your boat?").

Sentences: Negation and Emphasis

At almost any point, the student can review and consolidate what he has learned by relearning the same sequences with minor variations. Among the variants of the question and response sequences that he should be able to control are negation, emphasis, and probability.

Of these, negation is probably the easiest to elicit from an informant. In general, every affirmative response has at least one negative counterpart. The question "Is John here?" might be answered "Yes, he is" or "No, he isn't." Responses to content questions may have more than one negative counterpart. The question "Where is John?" might be answered negatively with "He's not here" or "No, John isn't here" or "He didn't come."

The student should also be alert to the possibility that a question can be asked in the negative: (1) "Isn't John coming?"; (2) "John isn't coming, is he?"; (3) "Is John coming?"; and (4) "John is coming, isn't he?" Notice that each of these forms has a different meaning, and calls for a somewhat different response. Check your own dialect of English to see what each of these questions implies, what kind of an answer it expects, and what kinds of answers can be given. Delicate differences of this kind cannot usually be elicited, but once the student is aware of some of the possibilities he may pick them up in natural contexts.

Similarly, emphasis ("I certainly will," "he really is") and probability ("maybe he went there," "I might do that") must be picked up in natural contexts. The student should look for special forms that accompany physical and social indications of anger, impatience, doubt, and hesitation. Once recorded, these forms can be checked with the informant for general meaning, or for appropriateness for various situations.

All drill, of course, should be in usable sequences. When practicing, the student should always trigger the stimulus sentence by imagining the context in which it might be said, and then let the stimulus sentence trigger the appropriate response. Negative stimulus statements, with their appropriate responses, may be used to review affirmation and response conversation types.

Clause Types: Transitive, Intransitive, Descriptive, Equative

All languages have some way of expressing the various kinds of relationships that are commonly called transitive (a subject doing something to an object), intransitive (a subject doing something without an object), descriptive (a subject described), and equative (a subject equated with another noun). The student should make sure that his inventory of stimulus sentences includes these four kinds.

Different languages have different ways of expressing these relationships. It is more important to discover the patterns that do occur than to impose patterns from English. For this reason, patterns elicited from the informant should be carefully checked in text. A pattern that has never been heard in natural conversation or found in recorded text should probably not be included in the lessons.

Transitive relationship is expressed in Mazatec by a transitive verb followed by a noun object and a noun subject: ti^{1}si^{1}te^{43} nio^4 čhǫ^{42} (is-making-wide tortilla woman) or "The woman is making tortillas." In Bororo there are two ways of expressing transitive relationship: (1) subject noun, transitive verb, object noun with an object suffix: ime e-rídí-re kii-ji (men they-see-past tapir-object) "The men saw a tapir"; and (2) subject noun, subject pronoun with tense marker, compound verb with the object included: ime u-re joro-go (men he-past fire-make) "The man made a fire." Note that in the second example the clause is intransitive in form, even though the English translation is transitive.

Intransitive relationships are frequently signaled by a subject and a verb: ti^{1}se^{43} ti^{34} (is-singing boy) "The boy is singing." There are many instances, however, of intransitive verbs which require some kind of complement. Verbs of motion are likely to require a locational or directional object; some action verbs require instrumental or accompaniment objects (for example, "cutting *with a knife*" or "running *with the dog*").

Description may be expressed, as in English, by a connecting verb and an adjective: "John is big." In Mazatec there are three different connecting verbs, one for weather or scenery, one for superficial appearance, and one for inherent quality: nta^{43} čǫ^3 nt^{ʔ}ai^{4}vi^4 (good is today) "It is nice weather today"; si^{3}ne^2 khi^3 ni^{4}se^{34} (yellow is bird) "The bird is yellow"; and nta^{43} ni^1 ti^{34} (good is boy) "He is a good boy." In many other languages the adjective functions as a verb, and may be indistinguishable from other intransitive verbs. Compare, for example, descriptive and motion intransitives in Maxakali of Brazil: kakcop pakígat (child sick) "The child is sick"; kakcop mǫ (child go) "The child is going." Some descriptives in Apinaye of Brazil may even be transitive and occur with an object: ixte kagą prąr (I snake brave) "I am brave with respect to snakes."

Equative relationships ("John is a man") may or may not require a linking verb. In languages where no linking verb occurs there are sometimes, but by no means always, special prefixes or suffixes on one or the other of the nouns.

As the student finds these patterns he should learn them in the types of conversational units that he is already using. He should be able to make an affirmation and response, a negative statement and response, a command and response, and all kinds of questions and answers using transitive, intransitive, descriptive, or equative clause types.

For each type, he should work through the reciprocal pairing of persons, and the equivalent pairing of tense or aspect. The range of possibilities, and the affixes used to express them, may vary considerably from one clause type to another. The student should not restrict himself to these four types if he finds others in his data.

Agreement of Units within Clauses

In English we are accustomed to changing the verb to match the subject of the clause. We say "I *am*," but "you *are*" and "he *is*"; "I *run*," but "he *runs*"; and "he *jumps*," but "they *jump*." If these are not matched corectly, the hearer may have difficulty in understanding. By the time the student has worked through the material suggested in earlier sections of this chapter, he will probably have noticed some quite different patterns of agreement or perhaps have been surprised by lack of agreement where he would have expected it. He can explicitly look for the patterns of agreement in material elicited from the informant. He should begin with a single sentence as a frame; each subsequent sentence should then differ by a single word. In each elicited sentence, he should check for all the changes that have occurred.

Exercise 3

Note the various kinds of agreement that would be explored by eliciting the following material.

(a) Elicit a frame sentence similar to the following: "The boy hit the tree."

(b) Test the possibility that different classes of subject nouns require agreement in the verb:

> The girl hit the tree.
> The dog hit the tree.
> The stone hit the tree.

(c) Test the possibility that the number of the subject requires agreement in the verb:

> Many boys hit the tree.
> Two boys hit the tree.
> Two girls hit the tree.
> Many girls hit the tree.

(d) Test the possibility that different classes of nouns as objects require agreement in the verb:

> The boy hit the tree.
> The boy hit the girl.
> The boy hit the dog.
> The boy hit the stone.

(e) Test the possibility that number of the object requires agreement in the verb:

> The boy hit the tree.
> The boy hit two trees.
> The boy hit many trees.

(f) Test the possibility that person of subject or object requires agreement in the verb:

> I hit the tree.
> You hit the tree.
> We (you and I) hit the tree.
> We (someone else and I) hit the tree.
> The boy hit me.
> The boy hit you.
> The boy hit us (including you).
> The boy hit us (not including you).

(g) Think of other kinds of agreement that might be tested.

Expanded Clauses

Up to this point, we have been talking about clauses in their nuclear or minimum forms—subject, predicate, and object. The content questions "where" and "when" have already implied other elements such as directionals (to _____, from _____), locationals (at home, in the water), and temporals (yesterday, early); such elements have occurred in the answers to the questions. In addition to these, most languages have slots for adverbial elements that express the manner in which an action was performed, and for indirect objects of various kinds.

The student should deliberately look for these and work them into his conversational sequences wherever they are appropriate. He may get some examples of expanded clauses from the natural conversation and other text that he has recorded: these can be amplified by eliciting from an informant.

It is important to note: (1) how many different expansion positions can occur in a single sentence (for example, time and place, or manner, time and indirect object); (2) in what order they occur and if a change of order signals a change of meaning or emphasis; (3) what the various items are that can be substituted for each other in a particular position (for example, the words "fast," "slowly," and "well," in a manner slot); (4) when one item is substituted for another, if there are corresponding changes elsewhere in the clause (for example, change of tense when the word "yesterday" is substituted for the word "tomorrow").

A few kinds of expanded clauses may be illustrated from Bororo as follows: (1) indirect object expansion: imedí u-re pébé makí **u-man-ai** (man he-past water give **his-brother-to**) "The man gave water to his brother"; (2) adverbial expansion: imedí u-re joro-go **pugeje** (man he-past fire-make **again**) "The man made fire again"; (3) directional expansion: i-tu-re **baakurirewï kae** (I-go-past **cuiaba toward**) "I went to

Cuiaba"; and (4) locational expansion: ime e-rĩdĩ́-re kii-ji **pëbë-të** (men they-see-past tapir-object **water-in**) "The men saw a tapir in the water."

Phrases

As the student works out substitution items for the various positions in clauses (subjects, predicates, objects, temporals, directionals, positionals, indirect objects) he will notice that many of these items have an internal structure of their own. This structure can also be described as a series of positions with sets of mutually substitutable fillers. In general, phrases are of three basic kinds: relator-axis, head-modifier, and coordinate.

Prepositional phrases in English are of the relator–axis type. The preposition is the relator and the following noun phrase is the axis—for example, "in" (relator), "the store" (axis). Relator–axis phrases from the Bororo examples in the preceding section include: u-man ai, "his-brother" (axis), "to" (relator); baakurirewĩ kae, "Cuiaba" (axis), "toward" (relator); pëbë-të "water" (axis), "in" (relator).

Many noun phrases in English are of the head–modifier type: "the" (article modifier), "boy" (head); "green" (adjective modifier), "grass" (head); "this" (deictic modifier), "table" (head). Similar examples were noted in Mazatec in an earlier section: hnko³ čo⁴ta⁴, "one" (numeral modifier), "person" (head); čo⁴ta⁴ yo⁴ma⁴, "person" (head), "poor" (adjective modifier).

Possessive phrases may also be thought of as a head-modifier type: "John's" (possessive modifier), "book" (head). Mazatec possessive phrases are quite different from English: na⁴-le⁴ ti³⁴, "mother-his" (possessed head); "boy" (possessive modifier), "the boy's mother." The order in Hishkaryana of Brazil is still different: meku y-erenĩ, "monkey" (possessive modifier), y-erenĩ, "his-liver" (possessed head), "the monkey's liver."

English coordinate phrases require the connector "and" (for example, "John and I," "boys and girls"). In some other languages two coordinate nouns may simply stand together without a connector, or the relationship may be indicated by an affix on one or the other of the nouns.

The phrase patterns should always be practiced and learned within the context of the conversational units. Many complete phrases were probably learned as indivisible units within sentences in early lessons. Once the patterns of internal structure have been discovered, they should be relearned with additional fillers for their various positions. For example, if the student learned to answer the question "Where is _____ ?" by saying "beside the river" or "in the house," he should now learn to say "in the river," "in the house," and "in the box," as well as "in the house," "beside the house," and "on the house." Similiarly, he might elicit a variety of modifiers and heads in the noun phrase.

In many languages it is difficult to decide whether some structures are phrases or words. For language learning this distinction is not very important: the student can find the positions, learn the appropriate fillers, and mimic the correct pronunciation without knowing whether the unit he is manipulating is a word or a phrase.

Complex Sentences

The student may discover some complex sentences by asking "why" and "when" (for example, "When will John come?" "He'll come when he finishes planting." "Why did John come?" "He came because his mother called him.") His inventory of complex sentence patterns can be amplified by trying to elicit sentences which express the following: "If _____ then"; "because _____ then _____"; "when _____ then _____"; "while _____"; "after _____ then _____"; "before _____"; "_____ and _____"; "_____ but _____."

In general, such sentences have two main slots, each filled by a clause, in addition to signals of the relationship. These signals may be conjunctions like English "and," "but," or "because," or they may be affixes on some word in one of the clauses. In some languages, certain complex sentences are made up of one clause followed by another, without any connector. In looking at the complex patterns, the student should check for the following: (1) What is the relator that shows the relationship between the two clauses? (2) Are there special verb forms required in either clause? (for example, "if I had gone _____" rather than "if I went _____"). (3) Do some nouns have to be left out of one of the clauses? (for example, "when John came, he saw _____" not "when John came, John saw _____"). (4) Does the verb ever get left out of one of the clauses? (for example, "If John goes to market, I won't" not "If John goes to market, I won't go to market"). (5) Which expansion slots can occur in each of the clauses? There is probably some limitation on locational, directional, and manner slots in one clause or the other.

Clauses within Clauses

In most languages a clause can occur within another clause functioning as subject, object, or modifier. At times these clauses have very specialized forms, but frequently they are almost unchanged. In English a clause as object or subject is quite modified. For example, in "I want John **to play somewhere else**," the object clause has the modified verb ("to play"); in "**John's playing here** bothers me," the subject clause has a modified subject ("John's"), and a modified verb ("playing"). Not all linguists would analyze these English sentences in just this way. Nevertheless it is important for the student to see a relationship between these special subjects and objects and the full clauses, "John will play" or "John is playing." In a new language the similarity to full clauses may be much more obvious and confusing if he were not expecting it. In some constructions, the included clause changes very little. For example, in "The boy **who wants to play**," the clause ("who wants to play") which acts as a modifier of "boy," is normal except for the special subject "who."

In any language, these patterns are likely to be rather rare. It is probably wiser for the student to learn them as he finds them in natural text, rather than attempt to elicit them from his informant.

Summary

The following is an outline list of the various kinds of grammatical patterns discussed in this chapter. It is not a list of universals; not all of these patterns occur in all languages. Nor is this list in any way complete; in whatever language he may study, the student will find many patterns that are not included here. The value of this list lies in the fact that it does include most of the kinds of patterns that are most frequently found. If the student were to control fluently this much of a language, he would be able to carry on a conversation easily. He would also be able to use this nucleus as a basis for learning the rest of the language.

Encounters

Openings (greeting sequences) and closings (farewell sequences) appropriate for various kinds of situations.

Conversational Units

Question and answer: Questions for confirmation that expect a *yes* or *no* answer, and questions of content.

Affirmation and response.

Command or request and response.

Sentences

The question, affirmation, negation, command, and response types required for filling the conversational slots.

Complex phrases such as: "if _____ then _____," "when _____ then _____," "because _____ then _____," "_____ and _____."

Clauses

Basic types such as transitive, intransitive, equative, and descriptive.

Expansions expressing time, place, direction, and manner.

Modified clauses within clauses.

Phrases

Relator–axis phrases such as: "to the place," "for the person."

Head–modifier phrases such as: "big cat," "run fast," "very sweet."

Possession phrases such as: "boy's mother," "girl's dog."

Words

Nouns. Affixes showing plurality, possession, or class (as the gender markers *o* and *a* in Spanish).

Verbs. Affixes showing tense, aspect, mode, person of subject or object, direction, or manner.

3

Vocabulary

TWO QUITE DIFFERENT kinds of vocabulary must be distinguished, as they are treated quite differently in language learning. Some vocabulary items belong to small, "closed" classes and are used primarily to signal grammatical relationships (for example, the English prepositions *on, to,* and *for;* the articles *a* and *the;* and the conjunctions *and, if,* and *but*). Affixes such as the plural *s,* the past tense *ed,* and the adverbial ending *ly* might also be thought of as belonging to this kind of vocabulary. The student should aim toward complete exhaustive control of these small grammatical classes, even though he learns only a few elements at one time. The control of person markers, plurals, and tense and aspect affixes is essential to the learning of word structure: the control of articles, deictic words, and prepositions (or postpositions) is essential to the learning of phrase structure; control of conjunctions is essential to the learning of complex sentences

The second kind of vocabulary items belong to large "open" classes such as nouns, verbs, or adjectives, and are used to signal lexical or dictionary meanings. These are called open classes because new items are constantly being added (for example, beatnik, fan-jet, sonic boom, televise, computerize, snap (take a picture of) electronic and galactic. No individual knows all the lexical items of his own native language, nor can he hope to learn all the vocabulary of a second language. This means that vocabulary learning must be selective. Chapter 2 outlined techniques for learning the grammatical structure with limited vocabulary; the balance of this chapter presents techniques for learning vocabulary within the grammatical framework.

Vocabulary in Context

Contrary to popular belief, the memorizing of lists of vocabulary is probably a hinderance rather than a help in language learning. Words are used only within the grammatical framework, and should be learned within that framework. We have already seen grammatical patterns as consisting of slots, each with a list of appropriate fillers. It is redundant to say that each vocabulary item fits in some slots, but not all (for example, we do not say "Run went to the store" (with a verb in subject slot), nor "John happy in the house" (with an adjective in the predicate slot).

Each new vocabulary item should be learned as a filler of a particular slot in a particular sentence. The daily lessons should normally include one or more frames with substitution possibilities:

Where did John go?   To the $\left\{\begin{array}{l}\text{river}\\\text{house}\\\text{field}\end{array}\right.$

When did you arrive?   I arrived $\left\{\begin{array}{l}\text{early}\\\text{yesterday}\end{array}\right.$

Words learned in one slot should be tested for appropriateness in other slots.

The $\left\{\begin{array}{l}\text{river}\\\text{house}\\\text{field}\end{array}\right\}$ is big.

Not all fillers of any one slot can be used in another place. We can say, for example, "I arrived early," "I arrived yesterday," and "yesterday I arrived," but not usually "early I arrived."

The student should be alert to the fact that the words of another language do not necessarily function in the same kinds of slots as their translational equivalents in English. In English, for example, various kinds of actions can function as nouns in subject or object positions: "*Love* is kind," "He made a *run*," "*Sleep* came slowly." In many other languages such words must occupy the predicate slot: "The person who *loves* is kind," "He *ran* to home base safely," and "He did not *sleep* for a long time."

It is not only important to use vocabulary items in the right slots, but they must be used in the right combinations; their meanings depend upon, or are modified .by, other words which accompany them. Note, for example, how differently the word "hen" is understood in the following sentences: "The old hen doesn't lay any more," and "The old hen is fifty if she's a day." Differences of another kind can be seen in the use of the word "run" in the following sentences: "He ran the fastest race of his career," and "He ran the car out of the garage."

The co-occurrence restrictions differ greatly from language to language. In English we may "bathe" the baby and "mop" the floor; in some languages one "washes" both. Mazatec, on the other hand, uses three different words for "is": "The weather *is* fine" (co^3); "The dress *is* pretty" (khi^3); and "The boy *is* good" (ni^1).

This means that the student should check the various co-occurence possibilities before he works them into his lessons and learns them. He should also be alert to note the specific words that native speakers use in different contexts. Observation is especially important in learning such contrasts as the following: "go" and "take" (from here to there) versus "come" and "bring" (from there to here) versus "fetch" (go from here to there and bring back). In Kaingang of Brazil, articles that are higher than they are wide are said to 'stand'; articles that are roughly as wide as they are high "sit"; and articles that are wider than they are high "lie." Such distinctions can be learned first as co-occurrence restrictions on certain words:

The $\left\{\begin{array}{l}\text{tree}\\\text{giraffe}\\\text{monkey}\end{array}\right\}$ is standing there.

The $\left\{\begin{array}{l}\text{chick}\\\text{ball}\\\text{basket}\end{array}\right\}$ is sitting there.

The $\left\{\begin{array}{l}\text{snake}\\\text{fish}\\\text{book}\end{array}\right\}$ is lying there.

Repeated observation may help the student to put individual words into categories.

To test vocabulary for co-occurrence possibilities, the student should set up a frame in which he keeps everything constant except the substitution items. Then he should test the vocabulary that he judges to be appropriate in that particular slot. In this testing he is asking, "Will this substitution item together with the frame make sense?" The following are the kinds of combinations that he should consider for testing: (1) various subjects with a single verb; (2) various verbs with a single subject; (3) various noun heads with a particular adjective; (4) a single noun head with various adjectives; and (5) particular verbs with locational or direction phrases. Setting up such frames is relatively simple, although the actual testing with an informant can be very delicate. If the informant is asked directly, "Can I say _____?" he may either reject everything for which he cannot at the moment think of as real life context or, on the other hand, he may accept everything which is grammatical in sequence of tagmemes without regard to whether the particular co-occurring items make sense in the language. It may be safer if the investigator, having lined up his frame and substitution list, elicited each item on the list from the informant by asking in the trade language, "How would you say _____?" If the form given by the informant did not match the material he had lined up and expected, he might then give his own version asking, "What would it mean if I said _____?"

There is another sense in which context is important in language learning. Each topic of conversation has some specialized vocabulary: smooth fluency requires the use of that vocabulary. A mention of fishing, for example, should bring to mind the related vocabulary (line, rod, hook, bait, catch) that permits the learner to participate in the conversation. Note that a number of words of the same grammatical class learned as a list (for example, fishing, hunting, paddling, catching, chasing, swimming, sweeping) will not stimulate a contribution to the conversation. A list of phonologically similar items (for example, fish, swish, wish, dish) will be of even less practical value in the conversational context. As the beginner adds to his vocabulary, he should do so in topical sets chosen for usefulness.

Areas of Meaning

There are very few, if any, vocabulary items that have a single, restricted meaning. Think of the word "apple." Did your first reaction to that word include "Adam's apple," "apple polishing," "crab apple," "apple green," and "the apple of his eye?" No word in any language is the complete translational equivalent of any single word in another language, as the secondary or peripheral meanings vary widely.

The student should use a new vocabulary only in the contexts in which he has heard it, until he has checked the usage in other contexts. He must be particularly wary of metaphorical meanings. Many English metaphors are so familiar that we have forgotten their metaphorical origin (for example, a "train" of thought, the "mouth" of a river, a "catty" remark). Translated literally into another language such metaphors are usually complete nonsense. On the other hand, the student should not be surprised to find unexpected usages in the language he is learning. The Mixtec language of Mexico, for example, uses parts of the body as locationals: "head" for "on"; "face" for "in front of"; "back" for "behind." In Mazatec, fingers and toes are the "beans" of the hands and feet. In Portuguese, *gato* ("cat") has the following secondary meanings: a person who is quick or bright; a clamp; a tool used by a barrel-maker; a mistake; a lie; a typographical error; a race horse of poor blood; and a thief.

Different cultures segment human experience in different ways. Color terms are a familiar illustration of this. Although all peoples see the same rainbow, not all languages have the same number of primitive color terms. The same colors represented by the six terms of English (red, orange, yellow, green, blue, and violet) are represented by three terms in Mazatec: ni^2 is used for red plus some oranges and some violets; si^3ne^2 is used for yellow, yellow-oranges, and yellow-greens; and sa^4se^4 is used for blue, blue-greens, and blue-violets. Green and blue are sometimes distinguished by referring to the sa^4se^4 of the sky versus the sa^4se^4 of the grass. On the other hand, Mazatec has primitive terms for each stage in the growth of the corn plant, for the corn grain in different conditions, and for different kinds of corn dough. It requires careful observation and sensitivity to local usage to speak clearly and precisely from the native speaker's point of view.

All languages have some hierarchies of terms which go from most specific to most general. In English, for example, a tiger is a particular kind of cat, which in turn is a particular kind of mammal, which in turn is a particular kind of animal, which in turn is a particular kind of living thing. To put it the other way around, in English we talk about living things in contrast to all nonliving things; animals in contrast to plants; mammals in contrast to birds and insects; cats in contrast to dogs, monkeys, or elephants; and a tiger as a particular kind of cat. Some languages distinguish domestic animals from game animals, and these from reptiles, by primitive terms. More surprisingly, at least one language groups birds, bats, grasshoppers, and airplane pilots as a single category of flying things. It is important to find these general terms and to find the specific terms they dominate.

The student can check the areas of meaning of any vocabulary items by asking his informant questions of various kinds. To determine the membership of an abstract category he may ask concerning a large number of objects, "Is this an _____" (for example, "Is a mosquito an animal?" "Is a dog an animal?" "Is a person an animal?" "Is a virus an animal?" "Is a cactus an animal?"). He can sort like items into parallel categories by asking "What is this?" (for example, "What color is this?" "What color is that?").

Word Shapes

In studying the vocabulary it is helpful to recognize the same item when it occurs in different shapes. Sometimes it is the whole word that changes (for example, "*a* table" but "*an* apple"); here "a" and "an" are two forms of the same word. More often, stems or affixes have different shapes when they occur in different combinations (for example, "wife" but "wive-s"). Some of the changes depend on phonetic environment. In English, for example, the plural suffix *s* is pronounced as: (1) a voiceless fricative [s] after voiceless consonants; (2) a voiced fricative [z] after voiced consonants or vowels; and (3) as a whole syllable [əz] after *s* or *z*. Pronounce the following plural words, listening carefully to the differences in pronunciation of the plural suffixes: cats, bluffs, tops; dogs, beds, knives; hoes, bees, laws; houses, mooses. (See Chapter 5 for a detailed discussion of the phonetic terms and symbols.) Not all change of form is dependent on phonetic environment; some of it is quite arbitrary. We say "boxes" and "foxes," *but* "oxen;" "houses," but "mice" and "lice;" "mooses," but "geese."

4

Sound Systems

THE BEGINNER learning a new language is faced with a bewildering stream of unfamiliar sounds, all pronounced—it seems to him—at extra high speed. In this confusion of noise, how is he to understand and reproduce what is being said? If, on the one hand, he recognizes and uses only the sounds which also occur in his own language, he will neither comprehend nor communicate well. If, on the other hand, he tries to hear and mimic all the phonetic detail, he will find it a discouraging job, and he may still fail to communicate.

The key to adequate communication lies in the discovery and use of the sounds which are distinct elements in the system of that particular language, and which are used to distinguish words. These elements of the sound system are called phonemes. A phoneme may have more than one variant, conditioned by its position in words or syllables, or by the sounds surrounding it.

These concepts can be illustrated by using examples of English words. Pronounce the words "tale," "dale," and "nail," listening carefully to your own pronunciation. Notice that the only audible difference between the three words is the difference between the sound of *t, d,* and *n*. This means that each of these sounds represents a separate phoneme in English, as each is necessary for a distinction between words. Now pronounce the following words: "Betty," "time," "stone." Listen carefully to the sounds represented by the letter *t*. Notice that the *t* of "Betty" is a very quick flap in which the tongue simply flips against the gum ridge. The *t* of "time" is a strongly aspirated stop. (Say the word "time" against the palm of your hand, and note the heavy puff of air that follows the *t*.) In the case of the word "stone," the *t* is not a flap; it is pronounced slowly like the *t* of "time," but has no puff of air. (Confirm this by pronouncing "stone" against the palm of your hand.) These three sounds of English (a flap, an aspirated stop, and an unaspirated stop, all made with the tongue tip against the gum ridge) are variants of a single phoneme, *t*. They are variants of one phoneme because although they are different from each other in ways which can be observed and described, they are never necessary to a distinction between words; there is no pair of English words in which the only difference is an aspirated *t* in one word and an unaspirated *t* in the other. The occurrence of each of these variants can be predicted, as they are conditioned by the phonetic environments in which they occur: the flap variety occurs between vowels; the unaspirated variety occurs following an *s* in a consonant cluster; and the aspirated variety occurs at the beginning of words. (This is not a complete statement of the complex distribution of the varieties of English *t*, but it will serve to show why the variants are not each a separate phoneme.) If the student is learning English, he must learn to pronounce these three variants of *t*; if they are pronounced incorrectly, the speech sounds foreign and peculiar. If, for example, the unaspirated variant is used in places where the aspirated variant should occur it may be misunderstood as a *d*, as happens in some foreign accents. The student would not have to strain to hear these differences in speech, however. He need only recognize any of the three variants as a kind of *t*.

In Mazatec, very similar phonetic data resolves into quite different phonemes: thi³ ("round") and ti³ ("boy") differ only by the difference between an aspirated *t* in one, and an unaspirated *t* in the other. Anyone learning Mazatec must not only make this difference in his own speech, but he must listen for it in the speech of others. The letter *d*, however, occurs only following *n* as in nda³ ("good"), and is a variant of *t*. The learner must pronounce the *d* in this position in order to sound natural, but he need not listen for it carefully in the stream of speech, as it is never used to distinguish words.

Finding the phonemes of a language requires some analysis. The analysis of the language learner, however, can be much simpler than that of a professional linguist. First, he needs only that measure of phonetic accuracy which permits him to make all the relevant distinctions, and to mimic acceptably; he can ignore much of the fine detail that delights a phonetician. Second, it will not seriously damage his language learning if he should happen to treat some variants as though they were separate phonemes. His most urgent problem is to find all the contrasts.

The following steps should provide a rough analysis, adequate for the purposes of learning a language:

1. Make lists of the same sound in the same position in several different words. The words should be of approximately the same length. The sounds that seem to be the same should be in the same position in each word—either first in the word, last in the word, or at the beginning of the second syllable. The following are sample lists of the English sound *p*.

Initial position in word:	pet	parsnip
	pill	pouting
	put	paring
	pound	
Final position in word:	loup	
	drop	
	keep	
	hardtop	
	catnip	
Between vowels:	upper	
	snooping	
	puppet	

Following "s" in consonant cluster:
spurt
spool
spelled
sputter
sparerib

Such lists will eventually have to be made for all the different sounds. Good procedure is to do the easiest and most obvious ones first, gradually adding the more difficult.

2. Listen to each list to decide if the sounds are really the same, or if some of them are different and belong on different lists. Be especially careful with pairs of words which sound exactly the same at first, but which the informant insists are different. There may well be a difference of a kind that the student has not been expecting, and has thus missed.

3. Compare the lists, looking for minor differences that correlate with a possible conditioning factor. In the four lists of English *p*, for example, careful listening will demonstrate that the *p* after *s* in the fourth list is always unaspirated; the final *p* in the second list and the intervocalic *p* in the third list are very slightly aspirated; and the initial *p* in the first list is heavily aspirated. This means that each of these is a variant of the one phoneme *p*, conditioned by its position in the word.

4. Compare all the lists of the same position. Again, look for possible factors that may be conditioning variants. Any sounds that cannot be explained in this way represent separate phonemes.

It is important to know that you do not have to have a pair of words distinguished only by a single difference in order to be sure that two sounds are separate phonemes. If they occur in the same position in a number of words, and if you cannot find any regularly co-occurring feature that could cause the phonetic difference, you must treat them as separate phonemes. In English, for example, it is very difficult to find a pair of words which are exactly alike except for the sound of *sh* as in "she" and the sound of *z* as in "azure." (The words *assure* and *azure*, which are very similar, have stresses in different positions.) These sounds are separate phonemes, however. This can be demonstrated by their occurrence in the following comparable positions, without conditioning factors: garage, menage, rouge, goulash, blemish, rush.

5

Phonetic Flexibility

THE STUDENT must be able to hear, produce, and write all the contrastive sounds in the language he is learning. In this chapter, emphasis is on flexibility in the production of sounds; once pronunciation of a sound can be consciously controlled it becomes relatively easy to hear and mimic it. In each subsection, the student is provided with a few fundamentals that he can use as reference points in locating sounds; an inventory of the most widely used sound types; and exercises designed to give him flexibility in recognizing and reproducing sounds.

In the exercises the words to be pronounced, and some tongue twisters are presented in ordinary English spelling. English orthography is not suitable for phonetic writing, however, because of its inconsistencies (for example, "to," "two," and "too" which are pronounced alike, versus "cough," "rough," "bough," "though," and "through" in which *ough* is pronounced differently). As each new sound is introduced, its phonetic symbol is given in square brackets; in some cases the phonetic symbol and the English letter are identical. This symbol is used whenever the phonetic quality is in focus.

For a discussion of phonetic theory or for more detailed consideration of particular sound types the reader should consult Pike (1943 or 1947); Hockett (1958); Nida (1950); or Gleason (1961).

Articulatory Positions

Seven major tongue and lip positions are sufficient to define most of the consonants that are common in the languages of the world. These positions, marked on the horizontal axis of the consonant chart (p. 58) include: bilabial (involving the two lips); labiodental (involving the lower lip and the upper teeth); alveolar (involving the tongue tip and the gum ridge); alveopalatal (involving the middle part of the tongue and the front part of the hard palate); velar (involving the tongue back and soft palate); and glottal (involving the vocal cords). The following exercises are designed to enable the student to "feel" each of these articulatory positions, and to control them voluntarily.

Each exercise for learning an articulatory position has five parts: part (a) is a tongue twister to be repeated until the position can be felt; part (b) is a list of words in which the consonants made at the new position are indicated in boldface type (these words are to be pronounced with particular attention to the similarity of tongue or lip position in the indicated consonants); part (c) is one word whose boldface consonant is to be prolonged (the other words of part (b) are then to be pronounced again, prolonging the boldface consonant in each case); part (d) calls for the student to think of rhymes for the given list of words. (Each rhyming word should begin with one of the consonants under attention. The student is to write the words using phonetic symbols for the initial consonants); Finally part (e) is a listening exercise. The student should record on magnetic tape a passage of normal English (read or spoken). He may use a single recording for all the exercises, or he may record a new passage each time. The exercise consists of listening to the tape for all instances of the articulatory position being studied. He is to write the word in which each articulatory position occurs, using the phonetic symbol.

Exercise 1: Bilabial Articulation

Bilabial articulatory position is used in English in the sounds represented by the letters *p* [pʰ], *b* [b], *m* [m], and *w* [w]. The superscript in [pʰ] indicates the aspiration of the initial *p* in English (see Exercise 23).

(a) Peter **P**iper picked a peck of pickled **p**eppers.
(b) **p** u **p** , **m** o **p** , **w** e e **p**
(c) a**pp**ear
(d) see, dark, lair
(e) Listen to your tape for the bilabial sounds, writing each with its phonetic symbol.

Exercise 2: Labiodental Articulation

Labiodental articulatory position is used in English in the sounds represented by the letters *f* [f], and *v* [v].

(a) **F**ive flippant fish fluttered funny fins.
(b) fine, vine, offer, over, fluff, above, suffer, sever
(c) fluff, above
(d) crumb, bore, meal, isle
(e) Listen to your tape for the labiodental sounds, writing each with its phonetic symbol.

Exercise 3: Dental Articulation

The dental articulatory position (in this case interdental) is used in English in the two sounds represented by the letter group *th*, as in the words "then" [ð] and "think" [θ].

(a) **Three** thirsty thinkers thought of thirty thorny thistles.
(b) thistle [θ], this [ð]; ether [θ], either [ð]; breath [θ], breathe [ð]
(c) breath [θ], breathe [ð]
(d) hiss, ink, nose, red
(e) Listen to your tape for the interdental sounds, writing each with its phonetic symbol.

Exercise 4: Alveolar Articulation

The alveolar articulatory position is used in English in the sounds represented by the letter *t* as in tin [tʰ] (see Exercise 23), *d* as in din [d], *s* as in seal [s], *z* as in zeal [z], *n* as in none [n], and *l* as in long [l]. (For flapped alveolar consonants, see Exercise 11.)

(a) Two tall taletellers told tall tales to two tired tots.
(b) teal, deal, seal, zeal, kneel [n], leave, eat, heed, piece [s], please [z], mean, eel, icing [s], rising [z], phoning, filing
(c) attitude
(d) frame, hero, brown, mend, fee
(e) Listen to your tape for the alveolar sounds, writing them with phonetic symbols.

Exercise 5: Alveopalatal Articulation

The alveopalatal articulatory position is used in English in the sounds represented by the letters sh as in "ship" [š]; z as in "azure" or g as in "garage" [ž]; ny as in "canyon" [ñ]; and y as in "you" [y].

(a) **She** should surely ship the sheep shortly.
(b) glacier [š], glazier [ž], azure [ž], assure [š], garage [ž], goulash [š], canyon [ñ], senior [ñ], junior [ñ], you [y], year [y], beyond [y]
(c) azure [ž], assure [š]
(d) Instead of looking for rhyming words, simply list as many words as you can using alveopalatal consonants, writing each such consonant with its phonetic symbol.
(e) Listen to your tape for the alveopalatal sounds, writing them with phonetic symbols.

Exercise 6: Velar Articulation

The velar articulatory position is used in English for the sounds represented by *c* as in "come" [k], *g* as in "go" [g], and *ng* as in "sing" [ŋ]. (Note that in "sing," and usually in "singer," the *g* is not pronounced; only [ŋ] is heard. In words like "finger," however, there are two velar sounds, [ŋ] and [g]. The word "singer" is usually pronounced "siŋ-er," but "finger" is pronounced "fiŋ-ger.")

(a) **My** country cousin cooks custard in copper cups, and cuts codfish with copper cutters.

    (b) cot [k], got [g], cut [k], get [g], lack [k], log [g], lung [ŋ], backing [k], bagging [g], banging [ŋ]

    (c) backing [k], banging [ŋ]

    (d) Think of English words with [ŋ] in the middle and at the end. Think of words with [ng] in the middle. Find words beginning with velar consonants to rhyme with drool, ford, and boast.

    (e) Listen to your tape for the velar sounds, writing them with phonetic symbols.

Manner of Articulation

The manners of articulation which are basic to an understanding of speech sounds are listed on the vertical axis of the consonant chart (see p. 58). They include: stop, fricative, nasal, semivowel, lateral, and flap articulations.

Exercise 7: Stop Articulation

Stop articulation is the complete cutting off of the stream of air at some position in the mouth. English uses stop articulation at bilabial, alveolar, and velar positions: [p], [b], [t], [d], [k], and [g].

    (a) Pronounce the words "appear" [p], "attend" [t], and "account" [k]. Repeat the words, prolonging the boldface consonant in each case, and letting the air build up behind the closure before releasing into the second syllable: "Appp-pear," "attt-tend," "akkk-kount."

    (b) Pronounce the following words, noting the stop articulation of the boldface consonants: poor, bale, time, done, kill, game, mop, lobe, mat, maid, mock [k], leg.

    (c) Listen to a tape recording of a passage of English. Identify the stops, and write the words in which they occur, using their phonetic symbols.

    (d) Make a stop at the labiodental articulatory position. First pronounce the word "funny," noting the labiodental position of the [f]. Then repeat the word, closing the lower lip tightly against the teeth and letting air build up behind the closure before releasing to complete the word.

    (e) Substitute interdental stops for the interdental consonants in the following words: thick, thin, three. Use the steps outlined in part (d).

Exercise 8: Fricative Articulation

Fricative articulation involves friction at some point in the mouth. To produce the friction, the opening at the articulatory position is narrowed so that the air produces a hissing noise as it passes through. English uses fricative articulation at the labiodental [f] [v], interdental [θ] [ð], alveolar [s] [z], and alveopalatal [š] [ž] positions.

    (a) Pronounce the following words: affair [f], Athens [θ], assume [s], assure [š]. Repeat the words prolonging the boldface consonant and focusing on the amount of opening between the lip and teeth or between the tongue and the lips, gum ridge, or palate.

(b) Pronounce the following words, noting the fricative articulation of the boldface consonants: fault, vault, thing [θ], then [d̵], sing, zing, should [š], wife, five, with [θ], writhe [d̵], pass [s], garage [ž].

(c) Listen to a tape recording of a passage of English; identify the fricatives, and write the words in which they occur, using their phonetic symbols.

(d) Make a bilabial fricative [ɸ]. To do this, pronounce the word "pin" with the lips closed enough to make friction, but not closed enough to permit air to build up behind them. Be careful to use both lips to form this sound; do not slip into labiodental articulation. Be careful, also, to make the bilabial fricative smooth—do not make a stop and then release it into a fricative. Practice until you can say "Peter Piper picked a peck of pickled peppers," with smooth bilabial fricatives throughout. For further practice read a page of English, substituting a bilabial fricative [ɸ] for every *p*.

(e) Make a velar fricative [x]. To do this, pronounce the word "come" with the back of the tongue close enough to the soft palate to produce friction, but not close enough to permit air to build up behind it. Be careful to make the fricative smooth; do not make a stop and then release it into a fricative. Practice until you can say "My xountry xousin xooxs xustard in xopper xups and xuts xodfish with xopper xutters," with smooth velar fricatives throughout. For further practice read a page of English substituting a velar fricative for every *c, k,* or *ck* having the sound [k].

Exercise 9: Nasal Articulation

The nasal manner of articulation requires that the air stream be completely stopped in the mouth, but allowed to escape through the nose. For this purpose the velum, which shuts off the nasal passage during oral sounds is opened. English uses nasal articulation in bilabial [m], alveolar [n], velar [ŋ], and, rarely, alveopalatal [ñ] positions.

(a) Pronounce the following words, prolonging the boldface consonants and focusing on the escape of air through the nose: bloomer [m], lunar [n], junior [ñ], hanger [ŋ].

(b) In order to feel and to get conscious control of the movement of the velum, say sequences of sounds with quick shifts from oral to nasal articulation (for example: mbmbmbmb; ndndndndnd; ngngngng). In the last sequence of sounds it may help to think of the word "finger," but to pronounce repeatedly only the *ng*.

(c) Listen to a tape recording of a passage of English; identify the nasals and write the words in which they occur, using their phonetic symbols.

(d) Practice the velar nasal [ŋ] (which occurs only at the end of syllables in English) at the beginning of syllables. Begin by pronouncing "singer" as "si-ŋer." Then drop the *si* altogether, saying [ŋer, ŋer, ŋer]. Repeat this using the following words and phrases: hearing aid [heari-ŋaid], swimming eel [swimi-ŋeel], and running up [runi-ŋup]. Be careful not to let any [g] sound appear. Practice until you can say the names of the vowel letters *a, e, i, o,* each with a velar nasal before it.

(e) Nasals can be made at other points of articulation as well. Using a mirror, test your own pronunciation of the word "comfort." Is your lip already against your teeth ready for the *f* when you make the nasal sound? If so, prolong this labiodental nasal. Try to substitute a labiodental nasal for [m] in the following words: from, muff, vim, mauve.

(f) Using a mirror, test your pronunciation of the word "panther." Is your tongue already in interdental position for the [θ] when you pronounce the nasal? If so, prolong this interdental nasal. Try to substitute an interdental nasal for *m* or *n* in the following words: thin, moth, than.

Exercise 10: Lateral Articulation

The lateral manner of articulation requires that the tongue be at the alveolar point of articulation, but the air be allowed to escape over the sides of the tongue. It is used in English in the sounds represented by the letter *l* [l].

(a) Repeat the following phrase, "eleven lovely ladies looking lovely, looked lovingly at eleven lively lizards," until the lateral position of the tongue can be felt.

(b) Repeat the tongue twister, prolonging each lateral.

(c) Listen to a taped passage, and identify the laterals.

Exercise 11: Flap Articulation

Flap articulation consists of a quick flap of the tongue tip. It is used in American English in the sound represented by the *tt* of "Betty" [ɾ].

(a) Pronounce the word, "Betty," "attic," "fluted," "setting," and "writing," noting the quickness with which the tongue flips against the gum ridge.

(b) Try to produce this quick flap replacing the *t* in the following: a time, (a [ɾ] ime), a tale (a [ɾ] ale), a touch (a [ɾ] ouch). Repeat the nouns without the article: [ɾ] ime, [ɾ] ale, [ɾ] ouch.

Exercise 12: Nasal and Lateral Flaps

Both nasal and lateral flaps [ñ] [l̆] are common in the world's languages, and they occur in some dialects of American English. As their names imply, these sounds are nasals or laterals made by a quick flip of the tongue. The author's dialect has a nasal flap in the following words: funny, penny, honey, many, sunning; and a lateral flap in these words: Polly, hilly, willing.

(a) The student can check his own pronunciation with the help of a mirror by comparing tongue movement in the following pairs: Hetty, Henney; hitting, hilly; catty, canny. If the tongue movement in each case is a quick flap at about the same speed, the student is using nasal and lateral flaps.

(b) Compare the tongue movements in the following pairs: a **knee**, **honey**; hey **Lee!**, **hilly**. If the pairs are different with respect to the timing of the *n* and *l*, it is probable that the student is pronouncing "honey" with a nasal flap, and "hilly" with a lateral flap. (Note that high speed repetition of any of these words may result in a flap developing where it does not ordinarily occur in normal speech.)

(c) Further contrasts of tongue movement may be found in the following pairs of tongue twisters: (1) "Try talking with two talking talkers" [t] versus "The pretty kitty is biting the writing writer" [ř]; (2) "The knowing need not know needlessly" [n] versus "Funny Jenny is running with many a penny" [ň]; (3) "Large ladies looked long at larger lizards" [ľ] versus "Silly Willie is willing to bully Molly and Billy" [ľ]. If the contrast between flap and nonflap occurs in each case, this exercise should make it possible for the student to feel the difference.

(d) If the student finds that he does not have nasal and lateral flaps in his dialect of English, he should attempt control of the flap manner of articulation by attempting to make the medial consonants of the following triplets look alike (have the same timing) in the mirror: **Betty**, **Benny**, **belly**; **putty**, **funny**, **Polly**; **Hetty**, **hilly**, **honey**.

Exercise 13: Trill Articulation (Alveolar)

The trill manner of articulation is not included on the consonant chart because it it not normally used in American English. The student may have heard an alveolar trill [ř] used in the so-called "Scotch burr," a manner of pronunciation in which all *r*'s are rolled (trilled). As a child, he may have used it as a motor noise. The alveolar trill is produced by relaxing the tongue tip, so that a forceful stream of air causes it to tap repeatedly against the alveolar arch. In speech, the trill usually consists of two or three such taps.

(a) Practice making motor noises with the tongue tip until you can start and stop the noise at will.

(b) Pronounce the following words, substituting the trill [ř] for the usual [r] in each case: **very**, **furry**, **rather**, **running**, **poor**, **bear**. Practice until the substitution is smooth.

(c) Read a passage of English, trilling all of the *r*'s.

Exercise 14: Trill Articulation (Bilabial)

The bilabial trill [b̃] is produced by relaxing the lips in bilabial position so that a stream of air causes them to vibrate. This is another sound often used by children for a motor noise. It is also used occasionally as a sign of cold (written *brr!*).

(a) Practice bubbling the lips until it is easily controlled.

(b) Practice the following tongue twister, "rubber baby buggy bumpers," replacing each bilabial stop with a bilabial trill.

Exercise 15: Trill Articulation (Uvular)

The trilling of the uvula [R̃] is also used as a speech sound in some languages (for example, the *r* of some dialects of French). The sound is produced by the rapid vibration of the uvula (the little flap hanging down at the back of the mouth). This sound is often produced in the process of gargling.

(a) Practice gargling without water until the trill of the uvula can be felt. Continue to practice until it can be stopped and started at will.

(b) Use a uvular trill to replace the *g* in each of the following words: gum, [R̃]um; go, [R̃]o; geese, [R̃]eese.

Modification in Point of Articulation

The points of articulation have been presented in terms of seven major positions. It should be obvious to the student, however, that considerable modification of these positions is possible. In fact, the tongue can touch the teeth, alveolar arch, palate, or velum at an infinite number of points in a continuum. It is probably sufficient to consider these modifications in terms of three possibilities: a neutral position (the one we have been discussing), a fronted variety, and a backed or retroflexed variety. In the phonetic symbols a fronted variety will be indicated by a mark to the left of the symbol [<k]; a backed variety will be indicated by a mark to the right of the symbol [k>]; and a retroflexed variety will be indicated by a dot under the symbol [ḳ].

Exercise 16: Positional Modifications of Velars

The three positions can be illustrated by English velar stops.

(a) Pronounce the words "key" [<k], "come" [k], and "call" [k>]. noticing carefully the different tongue position in each case.

(b) Repeat the following words until the fronted velar position can be felt: keep, key, keel, keen, ski, mosquito.

(c) Repeat the following words until the backed velar position can be felt: call, caught, coal, coat, cone, coop. Write the phonetic symbols for the sounds represented by the boldface letters.

(d) Repeat the following words until the neutral velar position can be felt: cup, cut, come, cuspidor, calm, college. Write the phonetic symbols for the sounds represented by the boldface letters.

Exercise 17: Positional Modifications of Alveolars

The modifications of alveolar consonants include a retroflexed variety, as well as a fronted variety and a backed variety. Retroflexion involves curling the tongue back to more or less the position of the *r* in the word "run." This *r* is very much like the vowel of the word "cup," with the exception of the curled position of the tongue.

(a) Repeat the following tongue twister until the retroflexed position can be felt: "The reader rereads the written rhymes he's read repeatedly." In some repetitions, prolong the retroflexed consonant represented by the boldface letters.

(b) The fronted [<] alveolar position may be dental or interdental. It occurs in most dialects of English in the words "tenths" [<n] and "at this" [<t]. Say these words using a mirror to see the tongue position. Repeat them, prolonging the sounds represented by the boldface letters until the tongue position can be felt. Say the words and tongue twister of Exercise 4, substituting fronted alveolar consonants for the neutral alveolar consonants in each case. Write the phonetic symbol for each fronted alveolar you have substituted.

(c) The backed [>] alveolar position occurs in the phrases "hat check" [t>], and "fine judges" [n>]. Say these phrases using a mirror to see the tongue position. Repeat them, prolonging the sounds represented by the boldface letters until the tongue position can be felt. Say the words and tongue twister of Exercise 4, substituting backed alveolar consonants for the neutral alveolar consonants in each case. Write the phonetic symbols for the backed alveolars.

(d) The retroflexed alveolar position occurs in the words "tree" [ʈ] and "dry" [ɖ]. Using a mirror, check your tongue position in these words. Repeat them, prolonging the sounds represented by the boldface letters until the position can be felt. Substitute retroflexed alveolars for the neutral alveolar consonants in the words and tongue twister of Exercise 4. Write the phonetic symbol for each of these retroflexed alveolars.

Exercise 18: Positional Modification of Alveolar Flap

The alveolar flap may also have fronted [<ɾ], backed [ɾ>], or retroflexed [ɽ] variants. The fronted variety may occur in the word "pathetic" [<ɾ] or in the baby talk phrase "itty bitty baby" [<ɾ]. A backed variety may occur in rapid speech in the phrase "he caught a chipmunk" [ɾ>], and in the word "photogenic" [ɾ>]. A retroflexed variety occurs in "ratty" [ɽ] or "rating" [ɽ]: in some American dialects a retroflexed flap also occurs in "barter" and "party."

Practice the prounciation of each of these variants. Substitute each in turn for the flaps in the tongue twisters and words of Exercises 11 and 12.

Exercise 19: Positional Modifications of Laterals

Two positions are usually distinguished in laterals: a fronted variety which is usually called a "clear" *l* [>l], and a backed variety which is usually called a "dark" *l* [l<].

Use the phrases "she leaps" [<l] and "he likes" [<l] as samples for practicing the clear *l*. Use the words "call" [l>] and "cool" [l>] as samples for practicing the dark *l*. Repeat these words, prolonging the lateral. Substitute each in turn for the laterals in Exercise 10.

Exercise 20: Positional Modifications of Alveopalatals

The alveopalatal articulation may be neutral, fronted, backed, or retroflexed. Neutral position occurs in the words "shop" [š], "shocking" [š], and "chop" [č]. A moderately fronted position occurs in the phrases "with sheep" [<š] and "both children" [<č]. A backed position occurs in the phrases "a long shawl" [š<], and "black chalk" [č<]. A retroflexed position occurs in the phrases "her shawl" [ṣ] and "better chalk" [c̣] in some dialects.

Pronounce each set of phrases until the position can be felt. Repeat these phrases, prolonging the alveopalatal consonant. Substitute each modification in turn for the alveopalatal consonants in Exercise 5; write the phonetic symbol for the substituted sounds.

Voicing

Long before this point, the reader will have been aware that there are differences that we have not been accounting for (for example, the difference between *f* and *v* or *k* and *g*). This difference is a matter of voicing in some, but not all, American dialects of English. The easiest way to isolate voicing is to make the difference between voiced and voiceless vowels. Pronounce the word "ah." By placing the hand on the Adam's apple or voice box (the larynx) you can feel the buzz of the voicing caused by the vibration of the vocal cords. Whisper the word "ah." Note that the buzz has disappeared. Alternately speak and whisper "ah" until the vibration of the vocal cords is under control.

Complete control of voicing in the consonants is difficult for speakers of American English. In most dialects the voicing is very light; it begins late in an initial consonant, and stops before the end of a final consonant. In some dialects, stops are not voiced at all; instead, relaxed unaspirated varieties are used for the voiced counterparts of the voiceless aspirated stops. For these reasons, the exercises on voice will begin with fricatives.

Exercise 21: Voiced Fricatives

(a) Say the following pairs of words with hand on larynx, noting the continuous voicing of the first member of each pair and the break in voicing in the second member: either [đ], ether [θ]; over [v], offer [f]; easy [z], essay [s]; pleasure [ž], pressure [š]. If, in your dialect, the first of each pair is not voiced throughout (that is, if the buzzing stops for a moment), practice until you can keep the vocal cords vibrating throughout the entire word.

(b) Now try to get voicing throughout the initial fricatives. These are also given in contrastive pairs of voiced and voiceless: vine [v], fine [f]; veal [v], feel [f]; then [đ], thin [θ], zip [z], sip [s].

(c) Practice voicing in the final position: alive [v], life [f]; breathe [d], breath [θ]; size [z], lice [s]; garage [ž], posh [š].

(d) Substitute fully-voiced fricatives for all voiceless fricatives in a reading of a page of English text.

(e) Review the voiceless bilabial fricative [ɸ] in Exercise 8, part (d). Make a voiced bilabial fricative [β] by pronouncing a [b] with the lips open just enough to let air pass with friction. Pronounce the tongue twister, "Bring better babies to the better babies bureau," substituting a voiced bilabial fricative [β] for the bilabial stops represented by the boldface letters. Practice until each fricative is fully voiced and smooth.

(f) Review the voiceless velar fricative [x] in Exercise 8, part (e). Make a voiced velar fricative [ɣ] by pronouncing a [g] with the tongue open just enough to let air pass with friction. Pronounce the tongue twister, "The girl will gladly go get gum," substituting a voiced velar [ɣ] for the voiced velar stop [g] represented by the boldface letters. Practice until each fricative is fully voiced and smooth.

Exercise 22: Voicing of Nasals, Laterals, and Flaps

(a) The nasals in English are ordinarily voiced, although the voicing may be light at the beginnings and endings of words. Review Exercise 9, testing with your hand on your larynx to make sure that you are voicing the nasals fully throughout.

To make voiceless nasals, block the air from escaping through the mouth by using the appropriate articulatory position; now breathe out through your nose. Practice the words in Exercise 9 until you can say them smoothly with no voicing in the nasals.

(b) The [l] is also normally voiced in English. Practice the varieties of laterals in Exercise 10 until voicing is complete; then make a voiceless lateral by forming the *l* and blowing through it. Practice voiceless laterals in the words of Exercise 10 until they are smooth.

(c) The alveolar flap [ɾ] in Exercise 11 is voiceless. In some dialects of American English its voiced counterpart [d̆] is found in such words as the following: ready, riding, middy, buddy. Compare these words with the following words: petty, writing, pity, putty. Use the techniques suggested in Exercise 12 to determine whether your dialect has a voiced alveolar flap.

If your dialect has both a voiced and a voiceless flap, practice substituting them for each other until you can use either at will. If you do not already have a voiced flap, practice the words with a voiceless flap, attempting to keep the vocal cords vibrating uninterruptedly throughout the word. Practice the set with voiced stop, attempting to make a flap rather than a full stop.

Recognition of contrasts of voicing in stops is complicated by the fact that in some dialects of American English, voicing is not used to distinguish the voiceless stops (*p, t, k*) from their voiced counterparts (*b, d, g*). All dialects do, how-ever, have both aspirated and unaspirated voiceless stops somewhere in the system. Exercises for the control of aspiration, therefore, precede the exercise for the control of voicing in stops.

Exercise 23: Aspiration of Stops

In all dialects of American English, voiceless stops in word initial positions are aspirated; voiceless stops following *s* in a consonant cluster are unaspirated.

   (a) Pronounce the following words against the palm of your hand, and feel the puff of air that accompanies the stops written in boldface: time, ten, tale, tear, tall [tʰ]; pin, pen, pole, pain [pʰ]; cool, can, come, kill [kʰ]. These are aspi-rated stops.
   (b) Pronounce the following words against the palm of your hand, noting the lack of a puff of air: still, stall [t]; spill, spoon [p]; skin, scare [k].
   (c) Repeat the words of part (b), thinking of the *s* but not pronouncing it. Check each time against your hand to be sure that you are not aspirating. Continue to practice until you can substitute an unaspirated stop for an aspirated stop without thinking of the *s*.
   (d) Read a passage of English, using unaspirated stops where aspirated ones nor-mally occur.

Exercise 24: Voiced Stops

   (a) Find out whether your normal pronunciation of *b, d,* and *g* is voiced. To do this, pronounce the words "obey," "heady," and "ago," prolonging the bold-face consonant. Keep your hand on your larynx, feeling for the vibration of the vocal cords. If the vibration stops abruptly, you are probably using an unaspi-rated voiceless stop rather than a voiced stop in these words.
   (b) If you do voice the stops, practice strong voicing throughout, using the fol-lowing words: boy, bee, abbey, oboe, hub, lab [b]; do, doe, heady, ado, add, odd [d]; guy, go, ago, eager, hog, rag [g]. Practice substituting voiceless un-aspirated stops in these words.
   (c) If you do not voice your stops in English, try to pronounce the following phrases deliberately keeping the vocal cords vibrating: we dare [d]; the berry pie [b]. To get the feeling of continuous voicing in this position, pronounce the following phrases, prolonging the voiced fricative: see there [ð]; the very pie [v]. Switch from the phrase with voiced fricative to the phrase with voiced stop until voiced stops can be said smoothly and with full voicing.

Glottal Stop

Up to this point we have discussed the vocal cords as either completely relaxed in voiceless sounds, or as vibrating in voiced sounds. They can also be completely closed to stop the air stream at the glottal point of articulation, producing a glottal stop. In English the glottal stop (here, indicated by a hyphen) occurs in the middle of the exclamation "oh-oh!" [ʔ]. It also occurs before a vowel in an initial position, especially if the first word is emphasized as in the example, "*All* the people went."

Exercise 25: Glottal Stop

(a) Repeat the exclamation "oh!-oh!," prolonging the stop, until the articulation can be felt.
(b) Pronounce the following sentences, noticing the glottal stop indicated by the hyphen: "I have to *re-eat it,* not *reheat it*"; "He said *a chapel* not *a-apple.*"
(c) Practice the tongue twisters of Exercises 1 through 6, substituting glottal stops for the sounds represented by the boldface letters.

Secondary Articulation

Consonant sounds can be modified by the following: (1) a puff of air (aspiration); (2) lip rounding (labialization); (3) tongue shift to palatal position (palatalizaton); (4) release into fricative articulation (affrication); and (5) preceding nasalization (prenasalization).

Exercise 26: Aspiration

Aspiration of stops has already been discussed in Exercise 23. That exercise should be reviewed in preparation for this one.

(a) Pronounce the following words against the palm of your hand, noticing the very light puff of air produced by the voiceless fricatives represented by the boldface letters: **th**in, **th**ree [θ]; **s**ee, **s**un [s]; **f**ree, **f**ill [f].
(b) Repeat the words, adding a puff of air to each fricative. Test your success by comparing the strength of the puff of air with that which is normal to the following words: tin, tree [tʰ]; pry, pill [pʰ].
(c) Read a passage of English, aspirating all the voiceless fricatives.

Exercise 27: Labialization

Labialization consists of rounding the lips as a consonant is pronounced usually with a transition sound similar to a *w,* following the consonant.

(a) Pronounce the following words, which begin with labialized stops in English: **tw**irl, **tw**irp, **tw**ist, **tw**inkle [tʷ]; **dw**ell, **dw**arf, **dw**indle [dʷ]; **qu**ick, **qu**irt, **qu**een, **qu**eer, **qu**est [kʷ]; **Gw**en, **Gu**atemala, **gu**ano, **gu**ava [gʷ]; **pu**eblo [pʷ]; **bw**ana [bʷ].
(b) Pronounce the following words in the variety of baby talk that substitutes a *w*

for an *r:* trunk, trough, trial, Troy [tʷ]; drag, drugs, drift, dream, draw, druid [dʷ]; crook, crazy, crow [kʷ]; green, gristle, grass, grace, group, grove [gʷ]; pretty, prance, proud, prone [pʷ]; bright, brother, bring, brood, brig [bʷ].

(c) Pronounce the following words which begin with labialized fricatives: swift, sweat, sweep, swarm [sʷ]; thwack, thwart [θʷ].

(d) Practice the labialization of fricatives by pronouncing the following words in baby talk fashion, substituting *w* for *r:* three, thread, thrice, throne [θʷ]; free, frantic, freight, fringe [fʷ]; shriek, shrink, shred, shrub [šʷ].

(e) Read a passage of English, labializing all the stops and fricatives.

Exercise 28: Palatalization

Palatalization consists of moving the tongue to position for pronouncing *y* as the consonant is being pronounced.

(a) Pronounce the following words that have palatalized stops: puny, pupil, pure, putrid [pʸ]; bureau, beauty [bʸ]; cute, cure, accuse [kʸ]; fuel, futile [fʸ].

(b) Palatalize the consonants represented by the boldface letters in the following words: pan [pʸ]; bare [bʸ]; tar [tʸ]; door [dʸ]; cool [kʸ]; gore [gʸ] ; thorn [θʸ]; than [ḏʸ]; fun [fʸ]; van [vʸ]; sun [sʸ]; now [nʸ].

A distinction should be made between an alveopalatal fricative [š] as in "assurance," and a palatalized fricative [sʸ]. In the former, the [š] has only one position; if it is prolonged there is no tongue movement. In the latter, there is movement from a neutral position for the [s] to the position for the [y]. If the palatalized [s] is prolonged, there is either a prolonged [ssss] followed by the [y] glide, or a short [s] followed by a prolonged [y].

There is an equivalent difference between the pronunciation of [ñ] without movement and [nʸ] with movement. A prolonged [ñ] is uniform throughout; a prolonged [nʸ] has either a long [n] or a long [y]. The student may discover that his normal pronunciation of "canyon" and "junior" is [nʸ] rather than [ñ]. In this case, she should now practice making the [ñ] required in Exercise 5.

Exercise 29: Alveopalatal Affricates

Affricated stops release into fricatives. Two of these at the alveopalatal position are used in American English: the first is the sound represented by *ch* in the following: church, chair, children, choose [tš]; the other is the sound represented by *j* or *g* in the following: jury, Jane, gym, gist [dž].

(a) Practice the alveopalatal affricates using the following tongue twisters: "Children chanting in church chant enchantingly," and "The jolly judge genuinely judged justly."

(b) Pronounce the following words or phrases, prolonging the stop, and then prolonging the fricative, so that the position of each can be felt: hatchet, eat chile, hat check, adjust, fudging, edge under.

(c) Read a passage, substituting an alveopalatal affricate for each *t* or *d*. Write the words, using the phonetic symbol for the affricates.

Exercise 30: Alveolar Affricates

The alveolar affricates occur in English as clusters of *t* with *s*, or *d* with *z*, as in the following words: cats [ts], adze [dz].

(a) Practice the alveolar affricates, using the following tongue twisters: "Betsy hates the bats and rats and cuts them into bits," and "He loads the hods, and pads the loads with pods.

(b) Prolong both the stop and the fricative release of the affricates in the following: pizza, cat's eye, kibitzing [ts]; adzing, toad's ear [dz].

(c) Read a passage, substituting an alveolar affricative for each *t* or *d*.

Exercise 31: Labial and Velar Affricates

Labial and velar stops can also release into fricatives at the same articulatory position: [pɸ], [bβ], [kx], [gɣ]. It is probable that the student actually made such affricates in his first attempt to make fricatives.

(a) Pronounce the following words, prolonging the stop represented by the bold-face letter, and following it with a prolonged fricative before finishing the word: a**p**art, re**p**eat [pɸ]; a**b**out, du**bb**ing [bβ]; ba**ck**ing, re**c**ant [kx]; bi**gg**er, be**g**one [gɣ].

(b) Read a passage, replacing every labial or velar stop with the appropriate affricate.

Exercise 32: Prenasalization

Stops and affricates may be modified by a preceding nasal at the same articulatory position. This occurs commonly in the middle or at the end of English words; the trick is to say it at the beginning of a word.

(a) Pronounce the following words, paying particular attention to the combined nasal and stop or affricate: co**mb**ine, ha**mb**urger [mb]; bi**nd**er, ca**nd**ied [nd]; a**ng**er, mo**ng**oose [ŋg]; a**ng**el, co**ng**eal [ndž].

(b) Think the first part of the words in part (a), but pronounce only the part beginning with the nasal: mbine, mburger, nder, ndied, nger, ngoose, ngel, ngeal. Continue practicing until you can pronounce the prenasalized stop in its initial position without thinking the preceding syllable.

(c) Read a passage, substituting a prenasalized stop or affricate for every voiced stop or affricate. Write each of the words, using the phonetic symbol.

Clicks and Glottalized Sounds

All the sounds discussed this far have been made with air from the lungs. Many languages, however, have some sounds made with air that does not come directly from the lungs. These sounds may be made with air from the mouth or the glottis. Mouth air sounds are called *"clicks"*; glottal air sounds are referred to as *"glottalized."* Clicks are more familiar to us, since they have at least marginal use in English.

Exercise 33: Clicks

(a) Make a kissing noise. Notice that the noise is made at a bilabial point of articulation by sucking air into the mouth. In the following words, substitute a bilabial click for the bilabial stops. Practice until the pronunciation of each word is smooth: pie, peace, cup, leap, supper, keeping, pop.

(b) Make the sound, usually written "tsk! tsk!," with which you reprove a small child. Notice that in this case air is sucked into the mouth at a dental point of articulation, making a dental click. In the following words, substitute a dental click for the alveolar stops. Practice until the pronunciation of the following words is smooth: tie, tease, cat, sleet, batter, seating, tat.

(c) Make the sound used for urging a horse to go. Notice that in this case, air is sucked into the mouth at a lateral point of articulation, making a lateral click. Substitute this click for *l* in the following words. Practice until the pronunciation of the words is smooth: lie, leaf, tall, peel, holler, feeling, lull.

(d) The clicks can be nasalized by thinking of an *m* while making the bilabial click, or an *n* while making the dental or lateral clicks. Practice these, using the words given above.

The glottalized sounds are not used in English, and so are more difficult to learn. They are formed by closing the vocal cords as for a glottal stop, and then moving the larynx up (to push air out) or down (to pull air in), while articulating a stop or fricative.

Exercise 34: Voiceless Glottalized Stops

(a) To make a glottalized bilabial stop, imagine that there is a tiny piece of paper or thread stuck on your lower lip. Hold your breath (closing the vocal cords) and try to spit it off. Put one hand on your larynx, and the other in front of your mouth. The repetition of the *p* motion made in order to spit off the paper should make the larynx pop up each time; the hand in front of your mouth should feel a short sharp burst of air. If you look in a mirror, the motion should look like a series of *p*'s.

When the motion can be controlled, it should be combined with a vowel in order to make a word. Try using it in the following words: pa, pay, pea, pow [pʔ]. It will make a tiny popping sound. Practice until it fits into the word smoothly. Then try it in these words: happy, supper, heap, trip.

(b) The glottalized alveolar stop [tʔ] can be made by holding the breath and trying to spit a bit of paper off the tip of the tongue, using the tongue against the upper teeth. Practice it in the following words: toy, tea, petty, eating, eat, bait.

(c) The glottalized velar stop [kʔ] may be achieved by holding the breath and attempting to clear a bit of paper from the back of the tongue. Practice it in the following words: coy, cow, sticky, looking, sock, book.

(d) By the time the student can make smoothly (as a speech sound) the three glottalized stops, he should be able to use the same mechanism for making each of the fricatives. These will be very weak, as the larynx does not provide enough air for strong friction. The student can constantly check whether he is using the larynx as a source of air by feeling its movement, or by watching for this movement in the mirror.

Exercise 35: Voiced Glottalized Stops

Voiced implosive glottalized stops are made by closing the vocal cords (holding the breath), and by lowering the larynx in order to draw air into the mouth. This is done while permitting just enough lung air to leak, in order to obtain some vibration of the vocal cords when pronouncing a stop.

(a) To control the bilabial implosive [bᶜ], pronounce *baʔ* (the word "bat" with a glottal stop substituting for the *t*) many times in succession as rapidly as possible. When the glottal and the bilabial stops are approximately simultaneous the student will feel, or observe in the mirror, that his larynx is pulling down to draw air. At this point, the *b* will have a hollow popping sound. (Some children use this sound, or the velar equivalent, in mimicking frogs.) Practice until the sound can be recognized and controlled. Use this sound as a substitute for the voiced bilabial stop in the following words: ball, beg, rubber, abee, jib, lob.

(b) To control the alveolar implosive [dᶜ], repeat the sequence *doʔ* (the word "dot" with a glottal stop substituting for the *t*). Continue until you can feel, or see in the mirror, that an implosive is being produced. Use this sound as a substitute for the voiced alveolar stops in the following words: dough, death, bedding, cloudy, bad, hood.

(c) To control the velar implosive [gᶜ], repeat rapidly the sequence *goʔ* (the word "got" with a glottal stop substituting for the *t*). Continue until you can feel, or see in the mirror, that an implosive is being produced. Use this sound as a substitute for the voiced velar stops in the following words: go, gourd, logging, sagging, log, rogue.

Vowels

It is customary to describe the tongue position of vowel sounds in terms of a three by three matrix—three general tongue heights, and three tongue positions from front to back. These are given, with English reference words, on the vowel chart, This is, of course, a very simplified scheme, as there are an infinite number of possible tongue positions; the smallest change in the shape of the tongue in any one position can modify the resulting sound.

Exercise 35: Basic Tongue Positions

(a) To see what is represented by tongue height, look at a mirror and pronounce the following words: beating [i] (high); baiting [e] (mid); batting [æ] (low). Notice the successively more open jaw and lower tongue with which these words are pronounced. Contrast the jaw and tongue positions in "beating" [i] and "bitter" [ɪ]. These are both classified as high, but the [i] is more closed, and the [ɪ] is more open within the high position. Similarly, although the [e] of "baiting" and the [ɛ] of "betting" are both mid, the [e] is more closed, and the [ɛ] is more open.

(b) To see what is represented by the front and back tongue positions, look in a mirror and pronounce the following words: beating [i] (front); booting [u] (back). The high central vowel [ɨ] is a bit more difficult to find. It may occur in a very rapid pronunciation of the word "just" (for example, in the phrase "just a minute") in dialects in which this is not identical with the word *just,* as pronounced in the phrase "a just judge." In some dialects, it occurs as the second vowel of the word "hatchet" when said at normal speech speeds.

Front, central, and back tongue positions can be seen at mid-height by looking in the mirror and pronouncing the following words: baiting [e] (front), butter [ə] (central), boating [o] (back). Notice that there tends to be a change in tongue shape as well as a retraction of the tongue as a whole.

Exercise 36: Vowel Glides

In most dialects of American English, there is a strong tendency to glide the vowel sounds (that is, to begin with one vowel quality and to end with another). Although there are a few relatively pure vowels (the "short" vowels or "simple" vowels of many descriptions), even these tend to be glided when they are prolonged. For this reason, one of the most important kinds of flexibility that the student needs is the ability to pronounce long unglided vowels.

Unfortunately, the glides vary in different dialects. The following exercises are based on the author's own Midwestern (Michigan) dialect. The student should look in a mirror to see how his own glides differ from those described here.

(a) Pronounce the following words in front of a mirror, noticing the way in which the tongue is raised at the end of the vowels: bee [iiˆ]; bay [ei]; bah (with vowel to rhyme with *bat*) [æə]; boo (uuˆ); bow [ou]; paw [ɔə], pa [aə]. Notice that [iiˆ] and [ei] finish with an [i] sound that is made with the tongue very close to the roof of the mouth very much like a [y]. The [ou] and [uuˆ] end with a sound similar to a [w]. The [æə], [ɔə]; and [aə] tend to end with the [ə] sound which occurs in words like "cut" or "but."

(b) Pronounce the word *bay* very slowly while looking in the mirror; note the shift from [e] to [i]. Repeat the word, prolonging the [e] before making the shift to [i]. Repeat it again, putting a glottal stop between the [e] and the [i]. Pronounce the word "bait," prolonging the [e] and then adding the [t] without slipping into the [i] position. Repeat this until the unglided [e] can be made consistently. Practice it in the following words: bait, mane, lame, paid, sale, crane.

(c) Pronounce the word *bow* slowly, exaggerating the glide from [o] to [u]. Repeat the word with prolonged [o] and shortened [u]. Repeat it again with a glottal stop between the [o] and the [u]. Pronounce the word "boat," adding the [t] to the [o] without slipping into the [u] position. Practice the unglided [o] in the following words: boat, moan, loam, abode, sole, crone.

(d) Repeat these steps with the following words: bah [æə], bat, man, cram, pad, pal, land; pa [aə], pot, on, Tom, pod, doll, clod; law [ɔ], lawn, bought, Paul.

Exercise 37: Flexibility of Tongue Position

This exercise consists of moving the tongue from one position to another, listening carefully to the sounds made at various points along the line of movement. This should help the student to locate and to recognize vowels that do not occur in English.

(a) Slide the tongue from the high front position [i] to the high back position [u]. Listen for the high central ɨ (represented by the boldface letters in "just a minute" and "hatchet," in some dialects). Listen for other varieties such as a slightly backed [i>], and a fronted [<u].

(b) Slide the tongue from high front [i] to low front [æ]. Try to lower the tongue still further; this should give the very low fronted vowel [ɐ] found in some New England pronunciations of "Bar Harbour." Stop the slide at your pronunciation of each of the English vowels on the vowel chart. Try to hear higher and lower variants of each of these.

(c) Slide the tongue from high back [u] to low back [ɔ]. Stop the slide at the position for each of the back vowels that occur in your dialect of English. Try to hear and pronounce the raised and lowered varieties of each of these.

(d) Slide the tongue from low central [a] to high central [ɨ]. Stop at the position for the mid central vowel [ə]. Try to hear and pronounce raised and lowered varieties of each of the central vowels.

(e) Choose other end points for tongue movement. Note the sounds through which the tongue passes (for example, from mid close front [e] to mid close back [o], and from high close front [i] to low back [ɔ]).

(f) Pronounce the pair of words, "bee" [i] and "boo" [u], several times; then put your tongue midway between them [ɨ]. Use this bracketing method for finding the following sounds that are not represented on the chart: a central vowel between [ɪ] and [ʊ]; a back vowel between [o] and [ɔ]; a central vowel between [a] and [ə].

Exercise 38: Lip Position

Exercises 35–37 focus on the position of the tongue. If you have been using a mirror, however, you may have noticed that the front vowels of English are usually said with the lips spread wide, and the back vowels are usually said with the lips rounded. The central vowels are somewhat more unrounded than rounded. This set of exercises is designed to disassociate lip rounding from tongue position.

(a) Repeat each of the slides suggested in Exercise 37, keeping the lips rounded. Listen for differences in quality when the front and central vowels are fully rounded.

(b) Pronounce the following words, rounding the lips for the vowels represented by the boldface letters. Notice the symbols for these sounds: seat [ü], sit [ü]. sate [ö], set [ö], sat [ɔ].

(c) Repeat each of the slides suggested in Exercise 37, keeping the lips spread wide. Listen for differences in quality when the back and central vowels are fully spread.

(d) Pronounce the following words, spreading the lips for the vowels represented by the boldface letters. Notice the symbols for these sounds: suit [ï], soot [ï], soak [ë], sought [ǽ].

(e) Read a passage of English, rounding all the front vowels, and spreading all the back vowels. Write each word, using the phonetic symbols.

Exercise 39: Voicing

All English vowels are normally voiced, that is, pronounced with the vocal cords vibrating. Occasionally, in some positions in some languages, the vowels may be voiceless or whispered.

(a) Repeat Exercise 37 without voice (that is, whispering). Listen carefully for the different qualities.

(b) Pronounce the following words, making the vowels represented by boldface letters voiceless, and the others voiced. Notice that the voiceless vowels may be written with capital letters: Blackfoot [U], heat wave [I], city park [I], lawsuit [U], coat rack [O], booked up [U], isotope [O], impeach [I], equip [I], best foot [E], blue plate [E].

Exercise 40: Nasalization

Nasalized vowels are made with some air escaping through the nose, and some through the mouth. Oral vowels are made with all of the air escaping through the mouth. In most dialects of American English, vowels are nasalized before nasal consonants, and they are oral elsewhere. There are a few regional dialects, however, which have a great deal of nasalization, while some individuals habitually "talk through their noses."

Since nasalization is often contrastive in other languages, it is important for the student to learn to control it.

(a) To discover which vowels you nasalize, pronounce the following words with your nose pinched tightly shut. Oral sounds will not be affected by the closing of the nose. Nasal consonants and vowels will have a muffled quality, and there will be a sensation of pressure in the nose. Repeat the words, prolonging the vowels represented by the boldface letters: meat, bean, beat [i] [i̧]; nit, pin, pit [ɪ] [ɪ̧]; flame, mare, flare [e] [ẹ]; [gem, met, jet [ɛ] [ɛ̧]; ham, mack, hack [æ] [æ̧]; come, mutt, cup [ə] [ə̧]; on, nod, odd [a] [a̧]; dune, nude, dude [u] [y̧]; home, mole, hole [o] [o̧].

(b) Repeat the words of part (a), nasalizing all the vowels. Repeat them again, making all the vowels oral. Practice until you can shift smoothly from oral to nasalized. Then make all of the vowels contiguous to nasal consonants oral, and all the other vowels nasalized.

(c) Read a short passage of English, first with all the vowels nasalized, then with all the vowels oral, and finally with alternating oral and nasalized vowels in each word.

Exercise 41: Laryngealization

When Americans (especially men) are tired, their voices usually drop from normal voicing to a quality called laryngealization. In this quality, the voice rumbles like a stick being drawn along a picket fence. In English, laryngealization may signal either weariness or boredom. In many other languages it is used to distinguish various vowels; it also functions as part of the basic sound system of the language. It is important, therefore, to be able to control this voice quality.

(a) Pronounce a prolonged vowel [a] at successively lower and lower pitch until the voice breaks into laryngealization [a̰]. Practice until you can laryngealize at will; continue practicing laryngealization with different pitches until you have gained good control.

(b) Read a passage of English, laryngealizing the vowels on alternate words. Re-read the passage, laryngealizing alternate vowels on each word. Continue to practice until a passage can be read in this way as smoothly as with normal quality.

Pitch and Rhythm

The student should be prepared to hear and mimic the pitch and rhythm of the language he is learning. These features are usually hard to control, but may be the most important elements in being understood. Each of the exercises in this section has been presented in two parts: The first part is to be done as a classroom exercise before going to the field; the second part is a list of suggestions for handling field data.

Exercise 42: Pitch

Part 1.　(a) English uses pitch in part to signal grammatical meaning, and in part to signal emotional meaning. Read the following sentences aloud:

> We went to the supermarket.
> We bought potatoes and ah, watermelon.
> You bought watermelon?

What pitches did you use in the first sentence to signal that you had finished? What pitch did you use on *ah* in the second sentence to signal that there was more to come? What pitch did you use in the third sentence to signal that you were not sure that you understood, and would like a repetition? Reread the three sentences, listening carefully to your own pitches. Hum or whistle the tune of each sentence.

(b) Read the following sentences aloud, saying each one as you would say it in the circumstances indicated:

> John, come here!　(frightened, wanting help)
> John, come here!　(angry, this is the third time you've called the child to lunch)
> John, come here.　(coaxing the baby to take his first steps)

Notice the different pitches and voice qualities that you use. Hum or whistle the tune of each sentence.

(c) Hum the tune of the following sentences: "I went to the market"; "I bought potatoes." Read the following paragraph, putting exactly this tune on each phrase that is set off by a solidus. This will cause each phrase to sound like a complete, finished sentence.

> Once upon a time/there were three bears/a great big father bear/a middle-sized mother bear/and a little tiny baby bear. The father bear/had a great big chair/the mother bear/had a middle-sized chair/and the baby bear/had a little tiny chair. The father bear/had a great big bed/the mother bear/had a middle-sized bed/and the baby bear/had a little tiny bed/just his size.

(d) Hum the tune of the following sentence: "You did go?" Reread the paragraph in part (c), using this tune on each phrase. This will make it sound as though you are asking for a repetition of each phrase.

(e) Hum the tune of the following sentence: "No I didn't but I could." Reread the paragraph in part (c), using the tune of "No I didn't but I could" on each phrase.

Repeat this exercise with other tunes found in your own speech, until you have developed easy control over your pitch patterns.

(f) Listen to a variety of programs on the radio or television, humming the speech tunes after the announcer or actors. Listen to some non-English programs, and hum or whistle the speech tunes.

Part 2.　(a) When learning a new language, spend some time each day listening to the pitch patterns, and mimicking them. Begin by trying to hum or whistle

the tunes; then try to mimic them. Use fairly short stretches for this purpose, so that you can repeat them many times.

(b) Mark the shape of the tune on each phrase or sentence elicited from an
informant. In general, it is good practice to write the consonants and vowels
first, then to ask for another repetition so that you can write the pitch.

Exercise 43: Rhythm

Rhythm is a matter of length of vowels or consonants, spacing of slight pauses or
rhythm breaks, and the like.

Part 1. (a) In English, the vowels before voiceless consonants are shorter than the
vowels before voiced consonants. Hearing and controlling this difference
will make it possible to hear differences of vowel lengths in other languages.
Practice the following words until you can pronounce aloud the part that
precedes the hyphen, and think the part that follows the hyphen, smoothly
and at normal speech speed. Then record the two sets of words on tape:
bea-ting, be-tting, hea-ting, bi-tty, He-tty; and bea-ding, be-dding, hee-ding,
bi-ddy, hea-dy. Listen to the recording, noting the difference between the
shorter duration of the vowels in the first set as compared to the longer
duration of the vowels in the second set. Mimic the recording.

Record the same words in sets as follows: He-tty, hea-dy; bi-tty, bi-ddy;
bea-ding, bea-ting; be-tting, be-dding; and bi-ddy, bi-tty. Listen to the
pairs, noting and mimicking the contrasts.

Record the ten words in random order, keeping a list of the order in which
they were recorded. Wait a day or two (until you have forgotten the order),
then listen to the tape indicating for each syllable whether it is long or
short. Check this against your list. Repeat this part of the exercise until you
can hear the length consistently.

Finally, practice making the pairs of words sound alike—both short, and
then both long.

(b) Long consonants occur in English within phrases when the final consonant
of one word is contiguous to the initial consonant of another word. Make
a tape recording of the following pairs of words: date time, daytime; wipe
pans, dry pans; freak cat, free cat; wise zebra, why zebra; eat chickens, see
chickens.

Listen carefully to the timing of the consonants represented by boldface
letters. Practice the contrasts until you can feel the difference in timing.

Pronounce the followings words normally, with a short medial consonant;
then pronounce them with a lengthened medial consonant: attack, appear,
echo, buzzard, satchel. Read a passage of English, lengthening each medial
consonant.

(c) Some languages put nearly equal timing and force on each syllable; others group several short light syllables and one longer heavier syllable together as a unit. To simulate this difference, record the following sequences. Pronounce the following words rapidly, one after the other: chair, put, hop, down, ten, pest, see, two, this, come. Read the following words as a normal English sentence: "I'll put the chair back in the room by the door when I come."

Listen to the recording, tapping out the rhythm of each of these sequences. The first sequence will have ten nearly equal taps. The second sequence will probably have four groups of taps, the first two having three quick light beats followed by a heavier one, and the third and fourth sequences having two light beats and one heavier one.

Record various readings, and tap out the rhythms. Record stretches of Spanish from a Spanish radio broadcast, and tap out the rhythms.

(d) Record the following pairs on tape, and listen to the differences in timing: the blackboard, a black board; any white house, the White House; nitrate, night rate; he ate up the bread, he ate up the street; I like tall men and women (the women are tall too), I like tall men and women (all women, not just tall ones). Practice making and hearing these differences in rhythm.

Record a stretch of non-English. Listen for the rhythm groupings. Try to mimic the rhythm.

Part 2.   When learning a new language, pay special attention to rhythm and timing.
(a) Listen to short stretches, noting any extra length of a vowel or consonant. Mimic what you have heard, paying special attention to length.
(b) Listen to short stretches of speech, paying special attention to the beat of light and heavy syllables. Tap out the beat and try to mimic it.
(c) Listen to short stretches of speech, paying special attention to the grouping of syllables or words, and the break in rhythm between the groups. Try to mimic this grouping.

Appendix

The following are minimal requirements for any tape recorder that is to be used for linguistic fieldwork:

1. It should be portable, and it must be capable of high quality performance.
2. Unless the student is sure that he will have reliable electric current, the machine should be powered by batteries. In many areas where electric power is available it is very unreliable; wide shifts in voltage may make it impossible to use a recorder, especially at the hours when there is a peak load on the system. In other places, there are frequent interruptions in power supply.
3. If he uses a battery-powered machine, the student should be sure that he has, or can buy, a sufficient supply of batteries. Flash light batteries are more widely available than larger batteries, but do not usually last as long. It is good to test the machine well ahead of time to find out how long batteries can be expected to last. It is also good to carry a small battery tester. Often the batteries that can be purchased in out-of-the-way places are old, and do not carry a full charge.
4. The machine should run at standard speeds so that the tapes can be used on other machines if desired. A good speed for fieldwork is 3¾ inches per second (ips). This is fast enough to give reasonable quality for listening and mimicking, but uses only half as much tape as a speed of 7½ ips. Although the 7½ ips gives better quality, it is not worth the extra expense. A speed of 1⅞ ips, on the other hand, is economical but probably too slow for best results; speeds slower than this should not be considered. It is important that the machine run at a constant speed. Some of the small machines developed for dictation purposes run faster when the reel is nearly empty, and slower as the reel fills. This makes it impossible to cut and splice tapes because of the distortion that results if they are spliced near the beginning or end of the tape.
5. The machine should have a hand brake, making it possible to wind the tape back by hand without stopping the motor. This is needed for repetition of the same item, and for elimination of the student's voice in recording. It is very difficult to manage

either transcription or selective listening if the tape cannot be rewound for short distances without stopping the motor.

6. The machine should be fitted with an earphone, so the student can listen to the tape without attracting an entire village to listen with him; it should also have a loud speaker, so it can be played for others. (Part of the technique of getting people to record is to allow them to hear their own voices.)

7. The microphone should be good quality dynamic ceramic.

8. The entire set of equipment, including the machine, the microphone, and the earphones, should be able to withstand the weather in the tropics.

9. A single channel one- or two-track machine is more useful than the more complex two- or four-channel machines used for stereophonic recording. When editing the recorded matter it is not possible to cut and splice the tapes if they have been recorded on two or more tracks. Therefore, a one-track machine is good; if a two-track machine is used, it should be used on one track only. (Although this system requires more tape—as each reel will record only half as much material as it would if both tracks were used—in the long run it saves time and effort and is therefore more economical than using two tracks.)

10. The machine should be the sturdiest available in order to withstand the travel and hard use.

11. The student should become familiar with normal care and repair of the machine. He should carry with him material for cleaning the head, as well as replacements for all fuses and small moving parts which may wear out quickly. He should learn and practice the care and operation of the machine before he goes to the field.

TABLE 1. CONSONANTS

	Bilabial	Labiodental	Dental	Alveolar	Alveopalatal	Velar	Glottal
Stops	p pin b bin			t tin d din		k come g gun	ʔ oh-oh
Fricatives		f fine v vine	θ thin đ then	s seal z zeal	š assurance ž azure		h oho
Nasals	m mother			n none	ñ canyon	ŋ sing	
Laterals				l love			
Flaps				ř Betty ḍ ready			

TABLE 2. VOWELS

		Front	Central	Back
High	Close	i beating	ɨ just a minute	u booting
	Open	ɩ bitter		ʊ butcher
Mid	Close	e baiting		o boating
	Open	ɛ betting	ə butter	
Low	Close	æ batting		ɔ bought it
	Open		a bottle	

References

Bororo

HUESTIS, GEORGE, 1963, Bororo Clause Structure. *International Journal of American Linguistics,* 29: 230–238.

Mazatec

PIKE, EUNICE V., and SARAH GUDSCHINSKY, Unpublished field notes.
PIKE, KENNETH L., 1948, *Tone Languages.* Ann Arbor, Mich.: University of Michigan Press.

Maxakali

POPOVICH, HAROLD, and FRANCES POPOVICH, 1961, Field notes. Rio de Janeiro: Archives of the Museu Nacional.

Zapotec

PICKETT, VELMA B., 1960, *The Grammatical Hierarchy of Isthmus Zapotec.* Language Dissertation No. 56. Baltimore: Waverly Press, Inc.

Bibliography

Language Learning

BLOOMFIELD, LEONARD, 1942, *Outline Guide for the Practical Study of Foreign Languages.* Baltimore: Linguistic Society of America.
CUMMINGS, THOMAS F., 1916, *How to Learn a Language.* Albany: Privately published by the Press of Frank H. Evory and Co.

FRIES, CHARLES CARPENTER, 1945, *Teaching and Learning English as a Foreign Language.* Ann Arbor, Mich.: University of Michigan Press.

JESPERSEN, OTTO, 1923, *How to Teach a Foreign Language.* London: George Allen and Unwin Ltd.

*NIDA, EUGENE A, 1950, *Learning a Foreign Language.* New York: Committee on Missionary Personnel, Division of Foreign Missions, National Council of the Churches of Christ in the United States.

PALMER, HAROLD E., 1917, *The Scientific Study and Teaching of Languages.* London: George G. Harrap and Co.

SWEET, HENRY, 1900, *The Practical Study of Languages: A Guide for Teachers and Learners.* New York: Henry Holt and Co.

*WARD, IDA C., 1937, *Practical Suggestions for the Learning of an African Language in the Field.* London: Oxford University Press, for the International Institute of Languages and Cultures.

Introduction to Linguistics

*BACH, EMMON, 1964, *An Introduction to Transformational Grammars.* New York: Holt, Rinehart, and Winston, Inc.

*ELSON, BENJAMIN and VELMA B. PICKETT, 1962, *An Introduction to Morphology and Syntax.* Santa Ana, Calif.: Summer Institute of Linguistics.

GLEASON, H. A., 1961, *An Introduction to Descriptive Linguistics.* New York: Holt, Rinehart and Winston, Inc.

————, 1963, *Workbook in Descriptive Linguistics.* New York: Holt, Rinehart and Winston, Inc.

HALLIDAY, M. A. K., ANGUS McINTOSH, and PETER STREVENS, 1964, *The Linguistic Sciences and Language Teaching.* London: Longmans, Green & Company, Ltd.

HILL, ARCHIBALD A., 1958, *Introduction to Linguistic Structures: From Sound to Sentence in English.* New York: Harcourt, Brace and World, Inc.

HOCKETT, CHARLES F., 1955, *A Manual of Phonology.* Bloomington, Indiana: Indiana University Publications in Anthropology and Linguistics, Memoir 11.

————, 1958, *A Course in Modern Linguistics.* New York: Macmillan Co.

LONGACRE, ROBERT E., 1964, *Grammar Discovery Procedures: A Field Manual.* The Hague: Mouton and Co.

NIDA, EUGENE A., 1949, *Morphology, the Descriptive Analysis of Words* (2d ed.). Ann Arbor, Mich.: University of Michigan Press.

PIKE, EUNICE V., 1963, *Dictation Exercises in Phonetics.* Santa Ana, Calif.: Summer Institute of Linguistics.

PIKE, KENNETH L., 1943, *Phonetics: A Critical Analysis of Phonetic Theory and a Technique for the Practical Description of Sounds.* Ann Arbor, Mich.: University of Michigan Press.

————, 1947, *Phonemics: A Technique for Reducing Languages to Writing.* Ann Arbor, Mich.: University of Michigan Press.

————, 1967, *Language in Relation to a Unified Theory of the Structure of Human Behavior,* 2d ed. The Hague: Mouton and Co.

*ROBINS, R. H., 1964, *General Linguistics: An Introductory Survey.* London: Longmans, Green & Company, Ltd.

SMALLEY, WILLIAM A., 1961, *Manual of Articulatory Phonetics.* Tarrytown, New York: National Council of Christian Churches.

———

*Recommended student reading.

Index of Symbols

(The first number refers to the page on which the symbol is found; the number in the parenthesis refers to the exercise.)

a	50 (36)		d^w	45 (27)
a^ə	50 (36)		d^y	46 (28)
ą	52 (40)		đ^y	46 (28)
ã̧	53 (41)		d^ʕ	49 (35)
ɐ	51 (37)		dž	46 (29)
æ	50 (35)		dz	47 (30)
æ^ə	50 (36)		e	50 (35)
ǽ	52 (38)		ei	50 (36)
ǽ	52 (40)		ë	52 (38)
ʔ	50, 51 (35, 37)		ɫ	52 (39)
ʔ̃	52 (40)		ȩ	52 (40)
b	34, 36, 44 (1, 7, 24)		ɛ	50 (35)
b̃	39 (14)		ɛ̧	52 (40)
ƀ	42 (21)		f	35, 36, 42, 45 (2, 8, 21, 26)
b^w	45 (27)		f^w	45 (27)
b^y	46 (28)		f^y	46 (28)
bb	47 (31)		g	35, 36, 44 (6, 7, 24)
b^ʕ	49 (35)		g	42 (21)
č	42, 46 (20, 29) [see also tš]		g^w	45 (27)
<č	42 (20)		g^y	46 (28)
č>	42 (20)		g^ʕ	50 (35)
ç̌	42 (20)		gg	47 (31)
d	35, 36, 44 (4, 7, 24)		i	50 (35)
đ	34, 35, 42, 44 (3, 8, 21, 24)		i>	51 (37)
ḍ	40 (17)		ii^	50 (36)
ď	43 (22)		ï	52 (38)

63